CELTIC SAINTS OF WESTERN BRITAIN

Celtic Saints

Of Western Britain

Nic Phillips

PUBLISHED BY AVALONIA
www.avaloniabooks.co.uk

Published by Avalonia

BM Avalonia
London
WC1N 3XX
England, UK
www.avaloniabooks.co.uk

CELTIC SAINTS OF WESTERN BRITAIN
ISBN 978-1-905297-87-0

Cover Art and all interior illustrations by Nic Phillips.

Design by Satori, for Avalonia.

British Library Cataloguing in Publication Data. A catalogue record for this book is available from the British Library.

About The Author

Nic Phillips is an English artist and writer with a degree in History and Archaeology from Cardiff University. He spent 12 years in Wales, before moving to Glastonbury, Somerset, to work at one of his most cherished heritage destinations, *Glastonbury Abbey.* Nic began exploring the landscape of the West Country from a young age with regular holidays in Cornwall which would eventually inspire some of the paintings herein and the book which followed. After illustrating two tarot decks with Kim Huggens exploring the Divine Masculine and Feminine, entitled Sol Invictus and Pistis Sophia, Nic developed his art on a larger scale. He launched *Nic Phillips Sacred Art* and studying and creating Eastern inspired icons, alongside depictions of the Goddess, as well as numerous saints, in a distinctive modern style.

All of the artwork in this book can be purchased as prints, cards, and more, directly from the artist through his website, Facebook, and Etsy store.

For more information visit:
www.nicphillipssacredart.com

Acknowledgements

This book came about through a love of the places explored within - to those who keep these sites sacred, I am eternally grateful. Its creation has also been possible through the encouragement and support of my parents, *Margaret and Paul Phillips, Matt Arathoon* for his love and belief in me, *Anna Dear* for her invaluable advice and inspiration, the help of *Ian and Gaynor Miller, Rob and Sonia Mortell,* the support of my long-term collaborator *Kim Huggens, Vanda Inman* and her insight on St. Clether's Holy Well, *Alan Rowland* for guiding me on a nail-biting cliff edge pursuit to Morwenna's Well, and finally *Sorita d'Este* for her friendship and belief in the project! To all my other friends who have shown their support through the book's creation, your faith in me is greatly appreciated.

I am also indebted to the works of the many scholars on the subject, particularly *Reverend Baring-Gould* and *Canon Doble* who compiled so much on the saints of the British Isles and who have influenced the work of almost every writer on the topic of saints ever since. This book is dedicated to all the saints I have encountered on my journey and in particular to the Archangel, *Saint Michael,* who opened the way to meeting the others.

Table of Contents

Foreword

This book is the culmination of a personal journey, scattered over several years. First visiting my favourite places in the South West of England, and later when I came to live in Wales, discovering some of the holy wells and pilgrimage sites of that part of the country also.

The paintings preceded the book, very much inspired by the special places I had visited, such as St Nectan's Glen, and St. Clether's chapel. I discovered a desire to not only illustrate the saints of these places, artistic depictions of whom seldom survive; but also, being a historian, I felt compelled to research and draw together the histories, folk tales, and customs attached to these figures. As such, this book does not comprise an inexhaustible source of every saint of Wales, Cornwall, Devon, and Somerset as that would fill many volumes! Selected in this volume are the figures whom I personally found provided the most interesting stories, or who had thematic links, some of whom you may be familiar with, and some I hope will be new to you.

Introduction

It is said that Cornwall is a county where one cannot take a step without tripping over one saint or another. Of the counties of the South-west, and even of Britain as a whole, Cornwall has by far the highest number of local patrons and churches with peculiar namesakes, often with little but the name remaining to tell us about these men and women who made their mark on Celtic Britain. Some, like Piran and Petroc, were more famed than others, and intricately bound into the folklore and customs of the South-west. Others leave only a name. Some, the reader may be surprised to find in Cornwall and the other counties of the South-west as their primary associations lie elsewhere. Saints such as Patrick and Brigid from Ireland, and David and Non from Wales; find their way into the legends and place names of this part of the country, as do the biblical figures of Joseph of Arimathea, and the Archangel Michael.

Many of these 'holy ones' set out from their native lands in search of seclusion rather than as missionaries, in the modern sense. The legends of many South-westerly saints begin in Wales and Ireland, from where the holy heroes travelled. Some were born of saintly parentage, more or less guaranteeing their path in life, and the persecution that went with it! As with the medieval preoccupation with the ancestry of the gentry, many attempts have been made over the centuries to record the lineage of the Saints. Many stem from great saintly families in Wales, giving them not only greater spiritual validity but also greater claims over territory for their churches and monastic houses. Wales, in comparison to the South-west, although also having many lone cult sites, has a much greater history of monasticism and evangelisation. The cult centres of St. David's, Llantwit Major, and Llancarfan, amongst others, were important wellsprings of education and critical in the formation of the monasticism of the Middle Ages.

Celtic Britain

When we talk about 'Celtic Britain' we refer to a particular time: after the fall and withdrawal of the Roman Empire, in the fifth and sixth century CE; and a place: largely the West and North of Britain. The regions of Scotland, Wales, and Cornwall, as well as Ireland and Brittany, are still widely identified today as being 'Celtic'. They were the last bastions to stand against the incursions of the Angles and Saxons from the east of Britain. And as such, the last places that still kindled the flame of Christianity after the retreat of the Romans.

However, the Christianity of the Celts did not marry up identically with the Christianity of the Vatican. Although the idea of 'Celtic Christianity' being distinct from 'Roman Christianity' is largely refuted by scholars today, as is the idea that there was a unified 'Celtic Church' which was opposed to Papal rule, the insular Christianity of these pockets of Britain and the local customs and traditions peculiar to them show distinct differences. Issues such as the dating of Easter set the Celtic Church apart. The Roman Catholic Church viewed it as more akin to Celtic Druidism, and certain ideas, such as the views of Pelagius, were regarded as heretical and distinctly pagan. Pelagius was, we are told, a Briton who believed that we are not born sinners and ruled by predestination, but that we have free will to either sin or follow Jesus' example. Differences in philosophy and the fact that many early monks may in addition have been schooled as druids are what set the Church of the Celtic lands apart.

In these areas, we find stories of a great many 'saints'. These are not the 'sainted', recognised on an international level as being canonised by the Vatican, but more precisely the 'saintly'; the title in this place and time referred more to a virtuous or holy person, or someone who died a good Christian (Rees, E 2001: 7). In fact, the only British saint recognised by the Catholic Church after the formalisation of Sainthood in the ninth century is Saint David.

Characteristics of Saint's Lives

The stories and legends regarding these saints generally arose several centuries after their deaths, when clerics decided to write the lives of the patrons of their parent monastery or church - and to fill in the gaps where known history was vague. We should not regard these *Lives*, or *Vitas,* as historical fact, since this is not why they were written. *Vitas* were intended to teach moral and spiritual values to the congregation, rather than recount a factual history of an individual. Their purpose was to reveal an idealised and virtuous life, attainable through Christ (Mullins 2002: 24). Although not dependable as sources of historical fact, particularly as many *Vitas* were written four to six hundred years after the time of the saints, they do give us valuable names and places (although sometimes mistranscribed) and probably used remnants of the oral tradition through which these saints' legends had previously been related. Although we can glean fragments of a forgotten age from them, more often they reveal more about Medieval attitudes than about those of their Dark Ages subjects.

The time setting of these hagiographies is a period of transition from pagan to Christian. Survivals of the pre-Christian age show through, sometimes in the form of adversaries to be banished - such as the dragon or witch - or converted, such as the archetypal wicked tyrant. Sometimes, however, the saints themselves show characteristics of their druidic predecessors. On occasion we find them stepping into the druid's role, blessing kings' armies and hurling curses at their enemies from hilltops. Often they expected to be afforded the same courtesies as their precursors such as grants of land, and should a pagan lord refuse them, they were inclined to fly into bouts of righteous indignation. The reputation of the saints as 'angry young men' is well documented and counterbalances the serene depictions of later ages.

Saints' *Lives* were mostly composed in Latin or Anglo-Norman and evolved from the heroic poetry and prose of the Anglo-Saxons, the heroic figure becoming a heavenly warrior rather than a secular one. Countless Saints' *Lives* feature their protagonists binding or exiling monstrous serpents; the successors of the dragon slayers of heroic literature. Some scholars theorise these episodes refer to a symbolic over-powering of the 'Old Religion', signifying a pagan tyrant or perhaps the wicker devices in which offerings were sacrificed to the fire.

The importance of the head rather than the heart is another Celtic survival which bleeds through into the *Lives* of the Saints. As with the head of the Celtic hero Bran which continued to talk after his beheading, heads of saints supernaturally survive, many of the stories featuring the saint's head being picked up by their still-mobile bodies and carried to a specific spot, usually the later site of their church. Heads were also the most important relics and were often kept separately in a box, highly prized and often stolen. For many centuries holy well water was supped from the skull of Saint

Teilo as a cure for various diseases and ailments.

Other tropes litter the *Lives* of the Saints, including the eliciting of springs which later became their holy wells, usually by means of thrusting their staff into the ground. Stories about the saints' association with wells, boulders, and hills are examples of topographical myths, giving us not only a show of their power and divine approval but providing us with an explanation for the origins of these sites.

Another example is the importance of animals in the *Lives,* which gives the latter day reader the impression that these holy men and women were more in touch with nature than their descendants and lived a more Edenic existence – where stags volunteer their services to plough a field when the saint's oxen are stolen, or wild hares shelter in the folds of the saint's cloak from the clutches of the gentry.

This book tells the stories of the popular and the lesser known saints of Wales, Cornwall, Devon, and Somerset, and where possible, gives the origins of these legends, using a combination of place name evidence, church dedications, archaeology, and literature. It will also provide the reader with a picture of the modern landscape of the Celtic saints, where to find some of their holy wells and churches, and hopefully the inspiration to seek them out for yourself.

Chapter 1

The Children of Brychan in Cornwall

Cornish tradition tells that a great many of its saints were of one family, and they hailed from the region of Brecknock in Wales, named for its patriarch, the ruler Brychan. The number of children fathered by this king varies greatly from source to source, from twelve to sixty-three and most commonly twenty-four. Many of these have their own dedications in and around Brecon, although Brychan himself has no churches dedicated to him and is often viewed as a patriarch rather than a saint.[1] Over time the transcription of the Welsh texts have produced duplicates, for example Goleu and Goleuddydd are thought to be one and the same, and Brychan's heir is listed as Rhain, Rhun, and other variations. Confusion in genealogies may have led antiquaries to include his grandchildren in the stated lists – Cadoc, Clydog, Mwynen, Gerwyn, Gwenan, Gwenlliw are amongst these.

Left: St. Nectan: Eldest sibling Nectan spent much of his time at the beautiful glen and waterfall now known as St. Nectan's Glen near Tintagel. The labyrinth pattern from nearby Rocky Valley is pictured here on a stone in the water. Acrylic on canvas board (19.5in x 27.5in).

---

1 For a time it was believed the sixteenth century 'Young Womens' Window' in the church in St. Neot, Cornwall, depicted Brychan with eleven of his children in his lap and was thus inscribed by its nineteenth century restorer, but this view has since been replaced with the belief that it depicts 'God the Father with souls in his lap' (Orme 2000: 77).

It may be that 'children' may have originally been intended to indicate grandchildren also, or even those that were 'of the House of Brychan', possibly the sons and daughters of other lords sent to his court. Rather than being blood kin they may have been 'brothers' and 'sisters' in Christ. It is clear from the medieval sources that they were of like mind, all living devout lives and sharing a desire for peace and solitude.

Brychan of Brycheiniog was born, most probably in the early fifth century, to the son of an Irish king, Anlach, and British mother, Marchell, the heir of what became known as Breconshire, when Marchell's father Tewdrig sent her to Ireland to procure a fur coat – and a husband! The fact of the matter may be that Anlach headed an invading force, but by taking a British wife was accepted by the locals, and set up home in the abandoned Roman station of Bannium, where Brychan was born.

As a young man Brychan was sent as a hostage by his father to the court of the King of Powys and it was here he fathered his first son, Cynog, on the king's daughter Banadlined. Welsh sources say Brychan had three wives, Eurbrawst, Rhybrawst, and Proestri with whom he fathered the majority of his offspring. Not all stayed local to Brecon, some settled in North Wales, Ireland, Scotland and France. Some went further afield, the sons of the Spanish Proestri returning to their mother's homeland. The twelfth century *Life of St. Nectan* tells us that the descendants of Brychan crossed the sea to Cornwall and North Devon to live lives of seclusion, most of their dwellings ranging along the North coast. Brychan's progeny listed by fifteenth century antiquarian John Leland as given in the *Life* are: Nectan, John, Endelient, Menfre, Dilic, Tedda, Maben, Wencu, Wensent, Merewenna, Wenna, Juliana, Yse, Morwenna, Wymp, Wenheder, Cleder, Keri, Jona, Kananc, Kerhender, Adwen, Helie, and Tamalanc.[2]

Nectan was named as the eldest of Brychan's children by the monks who wrote his *Life* at Hartland Abbey in the twelfth century. Hartland lies just over the Cornish border on the angular North Devon coast. Near the abbey in the hamlet of Stoke is a church

2 Leland's contemporary William of Worcester, writing from the calendar of the church at St. Michael's Mount records the names with the following spelling variations: Nectan, John, *Sudebrant,* Menfre*de*, *Delyan,* Te*th*a, Maben, Wen*t*u, Wensent, M*ar*wenna, Wenna, Julliana, Yse, Morwenna, Wym*i*p, Wenhede*n*, Cleder, Kery, Jona, Helye, *Lanant*, *Rer*hender, Adwen-*helye*, and Tamalan*t*. We can surmise such variations arise in the mistranslation of older handwritten texts.

dedicated to Saint Nectan where it is believed he set up his hermitage. The original church of St. Nectan, of which only the font still remains, is twelfth century. His well lies close by the church. A little further down the coast is another chapel dedicated to Nectan (or sometimes Nichton) at Welcombe, and another St. Nectan's church can be found near Lostwithiel in the south. His feast day is given as June 17th, the day he was martyred. The *Life of Nectan* gives us an account of his death, circa 510. After living peaceably on the North Devon coast for some years the two cows that gave him sustenance were stolen by robbers. Nectan tracked down the robbers and after taking back his cows proceeded to attempt to convert the men to Christianity. His teachings were obviously not welcomed as the robbers attacked him and cut off his head. However, the body of Nectan miraculously rose and, taking the severed head under one arm, slowly made his way back to the well at Stoke, his final resting place. It is said one of the robbers thereafter died and the other became blind and, filled with remorse, returned to bury Nectan's body. Where the blood of Nectan had fallen, foxgloves sprang up, and a tradition continued for many years of bearing foxgloves to his well on his feast day.

Another site further down the Cornish coast has legendary association with the saint. St. Nectan's Glen, found off the road between Boscastle and Tintagel is said to be another place he spent time as a hermit. Upstream in the Glen the stunning waterfall known as St. Nectan's Kieve can be found. Nectan's hermitage was said to be at the head of this waterfall although no evidence of it still remains. Legend tells that atop his oratory was a small bell tower, where he hung a silver bell which could be heard as far as the coast. The sounding of this bell was a comfort to seafarers who knew it was a sign that Nectan was about to pray for them. In his old age Nectan had become fearful that the light of Christianity was fading in the land. Before he died he decided that the silver bell should ring no more unless for a true believer. So standing above the waterfall, he asked for the bell to be brought to him. He rang it three times and then never again, casting it into the waters, prophesying that it would only be recovered by a true Christian. Shortly after this he died and two of his sisters came to bury him. They diverted the course of the river and buried him and his belongings beneath it in an oak casket, before allowing the water to return to its natural course. They continued to dwell there in solitude, apart from the occasional intrusions of curious locals, and there they eventually died within a few days of each other. Attempts were made in the following centuries to uncover the silver bell, all of which failed. One group were turned away by the sound of the bell ringing and a loud voice declaring "The child is not yet born who shall recover this treasure" (Hunt 1903: 278-82).

St. Nectan's Glen attracts many visitors to this day, and many tokens of pilgrimage or 'clouties' (pieces of material left in offering or in thanks for healing) can be found around the waterfall. The nearby Rocky Valley also attracts visitors to see the labyrinthine carvings on the rock which are thought to be sixth century, Nectan's time. Their significance, pagan or otherwise, can only be guessed. Interestingly the name of Nectan does not appear anywhere in the Welsh genealogies. However there is an Irish water god called Nechtan who had a sacred well of wisdom. Perhaps the Kieve's association with the saint of Hartland replaced an earlier dedication to a pagan deity? Nechtan may be a variation of another Irish god, Nuada, who is associated with British deity Nodens and the Welsh Nudd (pronounced Neath). In his book about Gwyn, the son of Nudd and master of the Wild Hunt and the Otherworld, Yuri Leitch brings the mystery full circle, noting the similarities in descriptions of the Vale of Neath and St. Nectan's Glen. Whatever the origin, the Glen today attracts as many, if not more, Pagan visitors as Christian.

The **John** and **Jona** of the list are likely to be one and the same. The north Devon town of Instow, originally Iohannestov, may have been associated with this John as early as the eleventh century.[3] John is a particularly confusing saint for many historians. Some believe him to be the patron of St. Ives in south-east Cornwall as the original Welsh version of his name may have been *Jeuan, Evan,* or *Ivo.* Some even associate him with the western and more popularly known coastal town of St. Ives, although this is commonly believed to originate from the female saint, Ia. The church of the Cornish St. Ive was thought to be dedicated to the same Ivo who gave his name to the St. Ives in Huntingdon, Cambridgeshire.

Endelient, Menfre, Dilic, Tedda, Maben, and Wenna all settled a little way inland, near to the modern town of Wadebridge. These six sisters lived in relative proximity to each other, perhaps for safety, yet appear to have lived solitary lives. Most of what little

3 Leland wrote from his twelfth century sources that John, son of Brychan, was buried near the River Torridge, opposite a chapel similarly dedicated. There was a chapel of St John across the river at Appledore. Any cult of this particular St John at Instow was replaced by the fifteenth century when the church was recorded as being St John the Baptist (Orme 1996: 173).

we know of them came from sixteenth-century antiquarian, Nicholas Roscarrock, whose family owned land in St. Endellion. He recorded local traditions of these and many other Cornish saints and is regarded as an early authority on folklore. He told how Endelient came into conflict with a local lord. The common people to whom she had shown kindness had given her a cow, on whose milk she subsisted. One day the cow wandered too far from Endelient's cell onto the land of the lord of Trenteny. Angrily the lord killed the cow which caused Endelient great distress. Furthermore, when news of this spread, Endelient's godfather (supposedly King Arthur) took great offence and slew the man who had dared offend his holy god-daughter. Naturally this did not please her and after much praying, not only the lord but the cow were both miraculously restored to life.

Endelient, presumably the most visionary of the sisters, had foreseen her own death. She ordered her body to be loaded into a cart drawn by oxen and wherever the oxen decided to stop would be where she was to be buried. Her tomb was apparently destroyed in the Reformation but later restored. Roscarrock believed she may be the *Cenedlon* (or *Cynheiddon*) that the Welsh genealogies list as a daughter of Brychan. She may have also had a retreat on Lundy Island, not far from her brother Nectan at Hartland[4].

The first recorded name of Menfre's church at St. Minver (her modern name) is in 1256, where her name appears as Menfrede. Not much is known about this saint although all accounts refer to her as female. One fabulous tale involves the well near her hermitage where she liked to sit and read her psalms. One morning as she sat in the sunshine, she put down her book in order to comb her hair. At this moment she was approached by Satan himself who had taken the opportunity to coax Menfre from her prayers. Not wishing to lose her only Bible, she instead hurled her comb at the Devil. It had the desired effect, and the touch of the holy Menfre's comb cast the Devil into the ground, creating a great chasm.[5]

---

4 The church on Lundy was later dedicated to 'Helen' which may be a misappropriation (Baring-Gould and Fisher 1907 vol.2: 452-3).

5 Roscarrock recorded her story, suggesting the chasm made by the Devil to be at Lundy Top (Orme 2000: 187).

Above: St. Morwenna: This painting brings together St. Morwenna on the cliffs of Morwenstow looking out towards her homeland of Wales, with the well that was dedicated to her in later centuries (right) and the 19th century Hawker's Hut and figurehead from the churchyard, iconic of Morwenstow (left). Acrylic on canvas (20in x 40in).

Merewenna and Morwenna are identified by some historians as being one and the same due to the similarity of their names and the proximity of their church sites.[6] These two saints, and also Menfre, have been suggested to be the Mwynen of the Welsh lists, a granddaughter of Brychan. She has also been confused by Leland, and later the Reverend Robert Hawker of Morwenstow, with Modwenna, a saint who died at Burton-on-Trent[7]. Merewenna is named at Marhamchurch, near Bude, from the eleventh century onwards. Morwenna was associated with the church at Morwenstow, on the north coast between Marhamchurch and Hartland, from at least 1201. Much of what is told today of the life of Morwenna comes from the writings of Reverend Hawker, whose eccentricities as well as his poetry became quite well known in the nineteenth century. Hawker's imaginative writing may also account for some of the details of her life, which may have been 'fleshed out' from his source material.

The legend goes that when building the church at Morwenstow, the saint carried the stones herself, from the shore and up the cliff, balanced on her head. From the spot where she stopped to take a rest, and put down the stone she was carrying, a spring emerged and this is reported to be the site of her well, which is now inaccessible to the general public, there being no actual path down the cliff and the whole thing being rather overgrown with blackthorn. The well itself was surveyed by The National Trust who decided not to attempt to create access, although the more intrepid explorer can still find the site, however the well has sadly dried up. The coastline here is quite perilous and in Hawker's time a great shipwreck killed all but one boy. The figurehead from the ship stood in the graveyard, and now in the church, in remembrance. Of all the siblings, Morwenna missed home the most, and when she was

---

6 Orme believes that Merewenna may be distinct from Morwenna and instead associated her with the English *Merwenn*, abbess of Romsey, as this part of Cornwall was one of the first to feature Anglo-Saxon settlements and the name may have been transferred here by the English (2000: 188).

7 Modwenna's *Life*, written by Concubran in the late thirteenth century, interwove the *Life* of an Irish Monynna, further confusing things. It was also greatly anachronistic, and tells how Modwenna taught Elfreda, the sister of Alfrid, son of the King of England. This was later taken by Butler and consequently Hawker to be Alfred the Great and his sister Edith, who lived in the tenth century, whereas Morwenna lived in the fifth. This massive anachronism was unaccounted for until late in Reverend Hawker's life, after it had already been depicted in stained glass at the church of Morwenstow showing Morwenna instructing St Edith of Polesworth (Baring-Gould 1888: 36-40).

dying, her elder brother Nectan came to minister to her. Her last request was that she be taken to the cliffs and turned so she could look out towards her homeland of Wales one last time.

Hawker, in his confusing of Morwenna with Modwenna wrote that she was born to Brychan and Gladwys[8], along with her 23 brothers and sisters, in the ninth century. She was brought up a noble and learned lady and was consequently sent for by the English king Ethelwolf to educate his sister Edith. After her time at court, Ethelwolf, pleased with her services offered her whatever she desired. She requested a plot of land to place a future church, which Hawker tells us is called a 'station' or stow in Saxon, therefore giving us his explanation of the name, 'Morwenna's stow' (1870: 5-7). Hawker held that the current church may originate from as early as 875, which he mistakenly regarded as Morwenna's time, but the earliest record we have is from 1201, and the earliest surviving material of the church is Norman, although its foundation on an earlier Saxon church site is possible. 84 years later in 1285 the church was re-dedicated to John the Baptist to coincide with it being given to the hospital of John the Baptist at Bridgwater, Somerset. Since then, both John and Morwenna's names are mentioned in church directories although never together unlike other co-dedicated churches (Orme 1996: 106). A medieval well of St. John stands in the grounds of the Vicarage and is not accessible without permission. Sources disagree about Morwenna's feast day, and it is variously stated as being July the 5th, 7th, 8th and November the 8th! Her feast day is not celebrated at Morwenstow, only that of St. John.

Cleder has been commemorated at the Norman church of St. Clether since the year 1249. The nearby chapel has the most complete and complex holy well in Cornwall. In the fifteenth century, the chapel was adapted so that the water from the well outside could be directed into the chapel to run beneath the altar. Here Clether's relics were interred, and the flow of water was thought to be given more healing properties as it passed over these remains into a further pool, until they were removed at the time of the Reformation. The chapel was in ruins by the late nineteenth century when the Reverend Baring-Gould headed plans to restore it. The chapel and well were re-roofed and returned as much as possible to the original design. The sturdy granite altar is thought to

---

8 Another inaccuracy as Gwladys was in fact a daughter of Brychan, not a wife.

be far more ancient than the rest of the fabric of the building, and bears five cruciform marks on it, signs of consecration (Inman 2005: 10).

This chapel served as the village church before the coming of the Normans. It was thought to be the spot where Cleder, who was reputedly called 'The Old' by the time he arrived, chose to base his hermitage. It is easy to see why, nestled in the Inny Valley it is a site of remarkable natural beauty even to this day.

Cleder, like Brychan, was something of a patriarch himself. He fathered twenty sons of his own while still in his homeland. Cleder's righteousness was renowned and in the *Life of Brynach* it is recounted how, before retiring to Cornwall, Cleder, or *Clechre*, as he is also named, humbly submitted his kingdom by the River Nevern to Brynach, his father's chaplain and confessor, leaving his sons to serve at his court (Orme 2000: 89).

He is believed by some to be synonymous with Saint Cleer, whose foundation also lies on Bodmin Moor, and is associated with the legend of the nearby stone circle, the Hurlers. Breverton reports that the saint saw some locals engaging in the sport of hurling on a Sunday. When they ignored the saint's chastisements for not going to church, he turned them to stone for their insolence (2000: 148-9). This type of tale served as a typical warning and explanation for standing stones in the Christian era.

Adwen is the patron of the church at Advent. The name of Advent was mistakenly thought to have arisen from the church being dedicated to St. Anne on an Advent Sunday in the eighteenth century, but it is clear that the place name comes from the earlier dedication to Adwen. Adwen is regarded as male in all but one source, but in modern times is often repeated as being female and the Cornish patron saint of sweethearts.[9] Her counterpart in Wales was **Dwynwen**, still celebrated today as the patroness of lovers. She was said to have settled in Anglesey near her sister Cain/Ceinwyn and we find her at Llanddwyn and Porthddwyn. The story of how she became Wales' answer to St. Valentine is that she loved a man named Maelon Dafodrill, who loved her in return.

---

9 Later dedications were made based on that one source recording the name as Adwena or Athwenna (Orme 1996: 67). William of Worcester's puzzling conjunction of Adwen with the following name Helye into one may be explained by the fact he had already interpolated Helye earlier in the list for some reason and would have ended up with one name too many, as suggested by Whitaker (1807 vol.2: 98).

Above: St. Clether: Pictured in front of the pre-Norman well and chapel on the site of his first foundation, Clether finds peace and a oneness with nature in the beautiful Inny Valley at the north edge of Bodmin Moor. Acrylic on canvas (16in x 24in).

However in his eagerness for her he took her by force, and as a result the appalled young woman rejected him. Nonetheless Dwynwen still loved him and prayed for the pair to be released from Love's spell. In a dream, her prayer was answered, and she was given a potion that cured her of her love, but turned Maelon to ice. She was also granted three requests. Dwynwen graciously asked that Maelon be restored to normal, that all lovers everywhere either gain the object of their desires or be cured of their 'love sickness', and finally that she never be married. Dwynwen's wishes were granted, and she retired as a hermit to Llanddwyn. Subsequently her well became a site of pilgrimage, not only as a cure for the sick but as a divinatory tool for lovers.[10] The movements of sacred fish that inhabited the well were said to predict the fortunes of lovesick

---

10 Llandwyn became a Benedictine abbey in the Middle Ages and the well was a popular pilgrimage site up until the Reformation. The Abbey and the well after became overtaken by windblown sand and inaccessible to all but the most determined seeker.

visitors when their lover's handkerchief was placed on the water. Similar prophesying took place in South Wales at Dwynwen's Cave, on the beach between Llantwit Major and St. Donat's, where throwing a pebble over an archway in the cave indicated the number of years until one was married, by counting the number of misses before getting a pebble over the arch. If the person was already married the number of misses equalled the number of years before they would be separated by death and free to marry another!

Helie is regarded in modern times as the patron of Egloshayle, since its dedication to Helie in the late nineteenth century. This is based on an assumption that the name of Egloshayle derives from 'the church (Eglos) of Helie'. However, names that begin 'Eglos' or 'Lan' are not always necessarily followed by the name of a saint. It is more likely in this case that the name means 'Church on the estuary' or salt marsh.[11] Helie may be identified with either *Heilim*, of the Welsh lists, who was male, or *Eiliwedd*, who was female. **Eiliwedd** was said to have run away from her father's court and the advances of a young Prince whom she was being pressed to marry by her family. She sheltered in the village of Llanddew but was not treated kindly. She moved on to the village of Llanfillo but in her poverty the residents mistook her for a thief. The inhabitants of the next village Llechfaen also treated her contemptibly so she sought out a hill, Slwch Tump near Brecon, to build a solitary cell and sought out the local lord's permission. Once settled, Eiliwedd cursed the inhabitants of the three villages in order, Llanddew with the Lord's chastisement, Llanfillo to be overrun with thieves, and Llechfaen to be struck with envy, for their ill treatment of her. Sadly, Eiliwedd's suitor found her abode and chased her down the hill, beheading her in a mad rage. Her head was said to have rolled the rest of the way down the hill, a spring issuing from where it stopped. She was buried in her cell which became a chapel. A similar desire to remain chaste and escape unwanted advances took Eiliwedd's sister Ceinwyn, or Keyne as she is known in Cornwall.

Keyne is an addition to the list of saintly Cornish immigrants who is unmentioned in the *Life of Nectan* but receives prominence

---

11 Before the nineteenth century and post-Reformation the church of Egloshayle had always been dedicated to Patrick, although pre-Reformation this was probably Petroc, as no other cult of the Irish Patrick existed in this area and this was an accepted sixteenth century spelling of Petroc (Orme 1996: 78). Baring-Gould associates Helie with the Welsh *Heilin* as mentioned in the sixteenth century *Peniarth* manuscript as a son of Brychan who had a church on Anglesey (1907 vol.3: 252-3).

in the list of Robert Hunt, a nineteenth-century writer.[12] He praises Keyne as the "brightest star" amongst her brothers and sisters and tells how she wandered the country in safety due to "the strength of her purity"; converting heathens, founding churches, and performing miracles wherever she went.[13] Keyne's future was well-omened, right from the start. When her mother was expecting her, a holy light shone from her breasts and she dreamt she nursed a dove in her lap, an omen of Keyne's purity. As a little girl her skin shone like snow in the morning sun. Nothing could sully her purity and as a young woman she refused all offers of marriage, preferring to stay virgin and dedicated to God. She eventually grew tired of the endless proposals from suitors and left her father's court seeking solitude. She crossed the river Severn and found herself in a rather inhospitable wooded country. Nobody appeared to be living for miles around, which suited Keyne just fine. After some searching she came across the residence of the prince who ruled the region and requested permission to settle there. The prince was rather taken aback at this and proceeded to explain to Keyne that no-one lived in that area as it was teeming with serpents. Even the wild animals avoided it. Keyne assured him that she could rid the place of the unwanted beasts, and, unable to refuse the holy virgin, the prince granted her strange request and bid her good luck. Keyne returned to the wood to face the writhing snakes, all the while praying in earnest to her Heavenly Father. Her prayers were answered as every serpent touched by her staff coiled up into a spiral and turned to stone.[14]

After some time in the area, news of Keyne's miraculous eradication of the serpents drew attention to her and she moved on into the South-west, settling at a crossroads, now the village of St.

---

12 Hunt begins Keyne's story stating that Brychan had 24 children and picks out several names quoted from the Leland and William of Worcester lists that have, according to him, churches in Cornwall in their name: "John giving name to the church of St Ive, Endellient to Endellion, Menfre to St. Minver, Tethe to St Teathe, Mabena to St Mabyn, Merewenna to Marham, Wenna to St. Wenn, Keyne to St. Keyne, Yse to St. Issey, Morwenna to Morwinstow, Cleder to St. Clether, Keri to Egloskerry, Helie to Egloshayle, Adwent to Advent, and Lanent to Lelant." (1903: 268-9). Nectan is missing, presumably because Hunt was writing only about Cornwall and not Devon where Nectan settled, and the rest because he was unaware of their cult centres.

13 Miracles are notably a later association with the saints. Before the formalising of canonisation, miracles were not a requirement for one to be called a 'saint'.

14 The story of Keyne subduing the serpents appears to be an explanation for the abundance of fossilised ammonites in the region which is now known as Keynsham, Somerset (Baring-Gould 1914: 178-9).

Keyne. Here she preached to passers-by, and remained to live out her days, except for pilgrimages to St. Michael's Mount on the south coast. When the time of her death came near she gifted the well near her home to the people who in return built her a church. This curious well was enclosed on all sides by four sacred trees – ash, oak, elm, and willow. Before she died Keyne imparted a prophecy on the well that when a couple married, whichever of them drank of the water first would retain the upper hand throughout their marriage, giving women a unique chance of dominance over their husbands. She had also blessed a rocky seat known as 'St. Keyne's chair' with the same virtue on one of her trips to the Mount.

The *Life of St Cadoc,* a twelfth-century piece about another grandson of Brychan, tells how he met with his aunt Keyne on a pilgrimage to St. Michael's Mount. Whether this was the Mont Saint. Michel of Normandy or the Mount in Cornwall as the story seems to imply, the story is anachronistic as the cult of the archangel had not reached either Normandy or Cornwall at the time of the sixth century when Keyne and Cadoc were alive (Baring-Gould and Fisher 1907 vol.2: 52-3). The Life tells how Keyne returned with Cadoc to Wales and settled at Llangeneu in Abergavenny, and elicited another holy spring, this one of healing properties. When she died two angels came down and exchanged her simple clothes for ones of fine crimson and gold, and afterwards she was buried there by St. Cadoc. Rice Rees identifies the St. Michael's Mount of this story with Skirrid Mountain, near Abergavenny, (1836: 154) although the Cornish Mount is more likely; the author of the Life seeming to show awareness of Keyne's cult in Cornwall and the people's reluctance to let her return to Wales.[15]

We know little about the majority of the other brothers and sisters in the Hartland list and the names that follow may have been corruptions of names from the Welsh lists, transmuted to the monks of Hartland through contact with Wales. Many have no obvious church dedications and it is unclear if they were venerated in Cornwall and Devon at all.

---

15 Besides the village of St Keyne, where she is honoured from 1291 onwards, the nearby St Martin-by-Looe jointly honoured St Martin and St Keyne between the sixteenth and twentieth centuries (Orme 1996: 101). There is also the parish of Kenwyn which may be derived from the Welsh version of her name Ceinwen (Cein the white or blessed). Her cult was widespread, with dedications in Camarthenshire, Pembrokeshire, Glamorgan, Anglesey, and Herefordshire.

Above: St. Keyne: This painting illustrates the fair-faced Keyne arriving in the wild forest where Keynsham now stands, and her miraculous petrification of the snakes abundant in the area. Acrylic on canvas (16in x 24in).

Juliana is possibly the patron of the church of St. Juliot, near Boscastle, and Lanteglos-by-Camelford. There is also a Norman chapel of Juliana on the headland at Tintagel, built over the remains of a much earlier chapel. There is confusion whether these dedications refer to the Welsh Juliana of the Hartland list or the Roman martyr Juliana, or even Julitta, mother of Cyricus, also a Roman. The origins of these dedications may have even been uncertain by the time of the Hartland list. The author may have assumed them to have been to the daughter of Brychan because of their grouping and proximity to churches of her brothers and sisters.

Yse has a possible two dedications, one at St. Issey and one at Mevagissey. The former is near the Wadebridge grouping. The latter is shared with St. Mevan, the name derived from Meva-hag-Issey: 'Mevan and Issey' in Cornish.

Keri has a church near to his brother Cleder at Egloskerry, the village name literally meaning 'church of Keri'. Keri may be the famed *Curig* of Wales who had many church sites but whose person later became mixed up with the Roman Cyriacus, son of Julitta, and displaced in many of his churches. (Baring-Gould and Fisher 1907 vol.2: 192-200).

Wymp is regarded to be the patron of the churches of Gwennap and St. Veep. Baring-Gould believed Wymp to be the Welsh *Gwenafwy,* who came via South Wales from the family of Caw of Prydyn, one of the famed 'three holy lineages' which also included Brychan's family (1914 vol.16: 246). Perhaps the author mistakenly attributed her to the wrong holy family?

Wencu is identified by some with *Nennocha,* a daughter of Brychan who went to Brittany rather than Cornwall and whose *Life* was composed and rewritten there. It tells how Brychan and a wife called Meneduc prayed for and bore a daughter after siring 14 sons, all of whom had left to preach the Gospel. She was given the baptismal name *Gwengustle* and fostered until she was of an age to be married. Following a visit from St. Germanus she resolved to live a virginal life rather than be married off and left for Brittany where she became abbess of a nunnery. Nennocha, or *Ninnoc,* means 'Little Nun'. Other variations of her name include *Guenguff* and *Vengu* (Baring-Gould and Fisher 1907 vol.4: 19). She is however unknown in the Welsh sources.

The only representation of **Wenheder** is alongside her sister Wenna in the St. Neot window. Baring-Gould surmises that Wenheder and Wenna may be the granddaughters of Brychan from the Welsh tradition, *Gwennan* and *Gwenlliu* (1888: 34). Other historians believe Wenheder to be the male saint Enoder who has a church at St. Enoder, but there is little evidence to clarify this.

Kananc is recorded by William of Worcester as *Lanant.* This has caused the presumption of many that the saint is the patron of Lelant, near St. Ives in south-west Cornwall, which was named Lananta from at least the thirteenth century. The church there was actually dedicated to Euny from that time but the name in fact indicates an earlier female patron *Anta* ('church site of Anta') (Orme 2000: 65). William of Worcester, presumably having knowledge of the parish of Lananta, translated the name thus and was followed by others in his misappellation. The fact that the parish lies so much further west than those of his/her brothers and sisters implies that it was a mistake. Kananc may in fact be *Canauc,* son of Brychan in the Welsh tradition, who Gerald of Wales described as owning a gold torc, which later became a relic on which many an oath was sworn, and which caused one assailant to go blind when he tried to break it. Similarly **Kerhender** is proposed by Orme as being the *Kenider* or *Cynidr* of the Welsh histories, a grandson of Brychan.

Tamalanc may be only a distortion of a Welsh name (not amongst the Welsh listed children of Brychan); and the only trace of **Wensent** is a family name at Lanteglos-by-Camelford, Fentenwensant which may indicate there once being a well (*Fenton* in Cornish) of Wensent nearby (Orme 2000: 252-3).

The *Life of Nectan* appears to be something of a conglomeration of church lists (many neighbouring parishes being listed consecutively) and corruptions of names from Welsh literature. It is possible some were locally born saints whose origins had been forgotten and who were then attributed to Brychan's clan. Although we may not be able to discover whether these saints really did come from one family, or whether they originated from Wales, at all what is important is the impact they had in this area of North Cornwall and Devon. Tradition holds that these twenty-four brothers and sisters gathered together only once a year, between Christmas and New Year, to give thanks and pray communally at the home of Nectan in Hartland. We can only wonder at what stories they would have to share with each other, fragments of which have passed into legend that survive to this day.

Chapter 2

The Irish Mission

If North Cornwall is known for its colonisation by saints from Wales, by contrast, South-West Cornwall is known for its abundance of Irish missionaries. The Irish immigrants who landed at Hayle may have set out to convert the Cornish, after their own conversion by none other than St. Patrick himself or alternatively they may have meant only to cross Cornwall on the 'Saints Way', an overland shortcut between Ireland and Brittany. This influx is alleged to have been all in one mission circa 460 CE, the band numbering 777. This number recorded in the *Life of Gwinear*, written circa 1300 by the monk Anselm at St. Michael's Mount, and including 7 bishops, is likely to be symbolic rather than historical. The number 777 is associated with holiness and perfection. The number 7 recurs in the Bible, perhaps being chosen to suggest the righteousness of their cause. Gwinear, who is also variously known as *Fingar* and *Guigner,* led the party that included his sister Piala. Upon landing in the Hayle estuary they met with opposition from the local king, Teudar, (variously *Tewdrig, Theodoricus*[16]) who slaughtered a number of their company, Gwinear amongst them.

Gwinear's story begins with his expulsion from the court of his father, Clito, after converting to Christianity[17]. About the time Gwinear reached manhood, his father received a visit at court from the great Saint Patrick. The young prince was the only one gracious enough to rise from his seat to greet the spiritual leader, and offer him his place. This story was, as we shall see, appropriated from

---

16 Interestingly the variation of Teudar's name, *Theodore,* means 'Gift of God' hinting at a Christian origin but we do not know if this was the original form of his name or a later alternative (Pascoe 1985: 22).

17 Rev. O'Hanlon believes the name Clito to be a misinterpretation of the name Olilt, King of Connaught (1875 vol.2: 674).

the deeds of Saint Erc. Nevertheless, Patrick's preaching made a lasting impression on Gwinear and several of his friends, who converted to Christianity. The apostle had less success with Gwinear's father, who was already old and set in his ways and had little time for the spiritual messages of his guest. Clito had even less time for his son, once he discovered Gwinear wished to become a follower of Christ rather than a warrior leader as was expected of him. Gwinear took leave of his father's court under a cloud and along with his sister and some of the other new converts set sail for Brittany. They were happily received and given permission to build a monastery on as much land as Gwinear could ride around in one day[18].

Once granted permission to settle, Gwinear went off alone, hunting. The legend tells how, covered in gore from butchering a stag, he searched for a spring to wash himself, and finding none, created his own by driving his spear into the ground. The story goes that on seeing his own reflection in the water, he remarked on how good looking he was, and that henceforth he would dedicate his own beauty to religion! He set about building himself a hermitage, vowing to withdraw from the world. His companions meanwhile had been arrested by the local prince on suspicion of murdering their leader due to his sudden disappearance. Given permission to find him, they searched the countryside and eventually were able to find his cell and bring the prince there, who dropped all charges. Gwinear was subsequently granted the land surrounding his cell, which Baring-Gould takes to be the large district of Pluvigner (1907 vol.3: 25-6).

On a return trip to Ireland, Gwinear found his father dead and his court looking to him to become their leader. His interests however lay only in the spiritual, not the secular, and he suggested one of their number marry his sister **Piala** and take the crown. However, the arrangement was not in Piala's interests either, as she had also chosen a religious calling, preferring to stay married to her faith. Piala, whose name is likely to be a Cornish 'softening' of the Irish *Ciara,* was adamant about leaving alongside her brother and their mission. Gwinear eventually relented and let Piala come with him, leaving the fate of his father's kingdom to chance, and leaving the chieftains to fight amongst themselves for supremacy. The

---

18 Baring-Gould supposes that the motif of leaving ones country to evangelise often covered up other reasons to emigrate, usually dynastic upheaval. (1907 vol.2: 25).

siblings roamed the countryside gathering willing Christians to join their mission and eventually amassed a group of 777, seven of whom were bishops. Notably amongst them were another king, Germoc, and his sister Breaca, who headed one fleet whilst Gwinear and Piala headed another. Anselm tells us that Gwinear planned to return to Brittany, but he and his party of 777 were blown off course and landed in Cornwall at the wide estuary near the modern town of Hayle. It seems unlikely that this was by chance, as even if their mission was set for Brittany- rather than Cornwall, they would have used the safer and more convenient overland route, already much trodden by traders, rather than going around the coast.

Gwinear's *Life* tells how his party stayed overnight at Connerton, just east of Hayle. Here they were accommodated by a good Christian, Conuria, who gave them her only cow to eat. Before moving on, Gwinear resurrected the cow and replaced the hay in her roof that she had given them for bedding. They moved south the next day and it was at this point they were tracked down by wrathful local king Teudar and his army, unhappy about this large band of Irish suddenly present in his country. Gwinear had gone ahead with a companion, to explore the land and at Tregotha he created a spring at the place where he planted his staff. Hearing the cries of the ambushed Christians, Gwinear backtracked to find his people being slaughtered by Teudar's forces. He fearlessly presented himself to the leader who wasted no time in beheading the saint. However, what Teudar did not expect was for Gwinear's body to rise, collect his head and walk away up the hill he had come from. It is alleged that here he came across a group of arguing women and, irritated by their abusive manners, cursed the spot to forever lie barren. He continued on, finding a spring in which to wash his bloodied head, before returning to the site of the massacre and finally expiring, eliciting yet another spring.

The bodies lay unburied where they fell, until a local man, Gur, had a dream vision about their whereabouts telling him to go to the site. Gur was reluctant and was discouraged by his wife from seeking them out in case he incurred Teudar's wrath. However the next day on a hunt, Gur's dogs drew him to the place of the attack and he was moved to bury the saintly men and women where they lay. Gwinear's church was later founded on the site of his martyrdom. These details, post-beheading, are thought to have been acquired from local legend and are not usually regarded as credible. Orme believes the author of *The Life of Gwinear*, Anselm, was likely to have been French, and the *Life* written for a Breton audience[19]. It is likely he drew upon an earlier Cornish version, as the details about Cornwall are far greater than the section about Brittany. The latter was probably added in to appease his audience and to associate him with Guigner the patron-saint of Pluvigner. The seventeenth-century writer Albert le Grand tried to compound this association by theorising that the events took place in Cornouaille, Brittany, and that Theodoric was a Breton ruler (Orme 2000, 136-8).

The fate of Gwinear's sister, Piala, is not mentioned by Anselm. O'Hanlon supposed her to be amongst the dead, but Baring-Gould theorised that she survived and was given land close to the site of Teudar's castle at Riviere on the mouth of the Hayle estuary in an act of repentance over the killing of her brother (1907 vol.4: 104). This is possible if we take Phillack church to have been named after her. However there is no record of the church ever being dedicated to her, rather to a 'Felec' which morphed into 'Felicitas' over time and to whom the church has since been dedicated. Anselm may have made the assumption that as Phillack parish bordered Gwinear parish it belonged to a close relation and therefore invented this sister and inserted her into his story, as his is the only mention of her (Orme 2000: 219). No other churches or chapel are dedicated to a Piala or any variation in Cornwall, Ireland, or Brittany. Despite this, the finding of an ancient phial of liquid discovered at the church is regarded as a relic containing the blood of Piala.

Teudar's actions represent the most curious part of their story. Was Teudar, as some have suggested, a fierce pagan king who mercilessly put to death followers of the new religion? Or is it possible he was in fact a Christian but on seeing such a large number of strangers appearing unannounced on his shores took it to be a less than peaceable arrival and chose to strike first in an act of self defence? The latter would explain why only a number were killed and the rest allowed to escape or given license to settle in the surrounding area which Teudar undoubtedly controlled, an idea supported by Pascoe (1985: 31). Whitaker wholly believes the king to have been a Christian and refutes Cornish antiquary William Borlase's hypothesis, that he slew a part of Breaca's company and all of Gwinear's, as being a wild exaggeration. He argues that other

19 This Anselm was later mistaken for St Anselm, Archbishop of Canterbury, and the *Life* therefore copied into a book of his works.

saints had preceded Breaca, and Cornwall was already somewhat Christianised. He may well have slain messengers thinking them to be spies, and the band of missionaries to be invaders or pirates (1804 vol.1: 331-4). This seems the most likely explanation; if he was a heathen there is no reason why he would not have killed all of them, rather than letting the rest escape and settle in the vicinity, lending their names to churches and parishes that still exist today.

Another saint's tale, The *Life of Petroc* tells of how the Cornish king Tewdrig kept a pit of snakes and serpents into which he flung criminals – and no doubt anyone else he took a disliking to. Tewdrig is described as being 'savage of manners' (but not *heathen* as we might expect to be noted if was the case). However Leland's account of Petroc says he was received in Cornwall by the pious kings Theodore and Constantine who granted him land for a monastery. This hints that the king, if it was indeed the same Theodore, was at some point a Christian.

What sources do seem to agree on is, whether pagan or Christian, Teudar was regarded as a bloodthirsty tyrant. He appears in the medieval play *The Life of Meriasek,* persecuting the saint (also known as Meriadec) who was thought to have been one of Gwinear's companions. In another saint's *Life*, that of Kea, we find Teudar as the king of a palace at Goodern, within the parish that later was named after Saint Kea. Teudar was annoyed at the saint for settling on his land and converting his people. One day Kea sheltered a stag that was being hunted by Teudar. In retribution he stole seven oxen and a cow from Kea, but the next day from the forest came seven stags and a hind to take on the ploughing duties. This further enraged Teudar who struck Kea, knocking out one of his teeth. Later in the story he repents and returns the cattle but then dies and his followers chase Kea from the land to Brittany.

The exact site of Teudar's palace at Hayle known as Riviere cannot be pinpointed, mostly due to the encroaching sands from the estuary which are said to have covered it even by the Middle Ages when Leland visited and recorded that Theodore's castle at Riviere was forever lost below the sand. A likely site is a little way up the hill at Phillack, the stone from the castle possibly being later reused to build the original parish church. The churchyard shows signs of having been built on a much more ancient site; part of its wall follows the curve of an Iron Age cemetery and burials dating to this period were unearthed. Whether this proves Teudar

Above: The Irish Saints: Here we see the landing of the many Irish missionaries in the Hayle Estuary, with St. Ives just visible in the distance. Breaca (left) leads one group south whilst Gwinear and Piala (right) head another party moving east. Acrylic on canvas board (16.5in x 23.5in).

was a Christian is unsure as no items were discovered with the bodies although they were buried lying east to west as is the Christian tradition.

Besides the *Life of Gwinear* we have information from the *Life of Breaca* which does not survive but was seen by Leland in his visit to Cornwall. He recorded that **Breaca** was born somewhere between Leinster and Ulster and that she spent time in a nunnery founded by St. Brigid in County Meath[20]. She came to Cornwall in the company of Sinnin, an abbot, Maruan, a monk, Germoc, a king,

---

20 Breaca's name is also variously given as Breage, Briac and Brig. Baring-Gould theorises several Brigs in the Irish annals as possibilities for her identity, including the Virgin Abbess of Killbrig and the friend of Senan, Brig, daughter of Cu Cathrach (1907 vol.1: 229). Many variants of Brig/Bridget exist at this place and time so it is near impossible to decipher her origin with what little information Leland left us.

and others, named as Elwen, Helena, Crowan, and Tecla. They landed at Revyer where some of the party were killed by Teudar before Breaca's company moved south. Borlase believed the landings and subsequent fates of this party and Gwinear's to have been at separate but similar times, an idea wildly refuted by Whitaker (1804 vol.1: 327-331). The similarities between the stories are so striking that the motif has either been entirely borrowed one from the other or the mission was one and the same; Breaca and Gwinear parting company and leading separate groups, one east and one south. Whitaker believed that there could not have been two missions, and that the details Borlase takes from the *Life of Gwinear* were not credible, believing the recordings of Leland to be more genuine than the writings of Anselm.

Escaping the swords of Teudar and his men, Breaca and her companions fled south, sheltering at the ancient fortification of Pencair on Tregonning Hill, before moving on to Trenewith, now Chynoweth near St. Hilary, and eventually settling at the spot that became Breage. Breaca has a central role as leader in the story but this may only be because it is, after all, her *Life* and would have been written at and for the church of Breage. However it is curious to find chapels dedicated to other saints, including the king Germoc, coming under the rule of the mother-church at Breage; especially when we consider the old local saying, reiterated by Robert Hunt: "Germoc was a king, Breaca a midwife" (1903: 267). Perhaps in this new and strange land her spiritual authority, coming from the house of St. Brigid, outweighed the rest and made her their natural leader? Hunt regarded Breaca as also being the sister of St. Levan and incorporates her into his telling of the story of Levan and the two fish (see Chapter 5), yet tells nothing further of her exploits.

Germoc was regarded by William of Worcester as being a bishop but whether this title was awarded to him before or after their embarkation from Ireland we do not know. What sources seem to agree on was his status as king, and on a visit to the village of Germoe, Leland found the saint's tomb, well, and chair in the vicinity of the church. A throne or chair is a peculiar thing to find in a churchyard so it is likely this saint's cult worship involved his aspect as a king.[21] W. H. Pascoe goes further to say that Germoc's

21 The tomb is now lost and the chair replaced with a more modern and grandiose version, reportedly donated by the Milliton family (Drew 1824 vol.2: 285).

status as king may have been what helped the missionaries escape from all being martyred by Teudar, perhaps not wanting to rouse the vengeance of the Irish people and provoke a second invasion, this time a less friendly one (1985: 35).

With regards to the abbot **Sinnin** it is claimed in Cornwall that he founded the church at, and is buried at, what is now Sithney. He is better known in Brittany where he is named *Sezni*. Breton tradition, recorded in the seventeenth century by Albert Le Grand, tells how he was born in Ireland and visited Rome and met St. Patrick (details agreed upon in the *Life of Breaca*) and was made a bishop by the Pope. He returned with Patrick to Ireland and founded a monastery, later travelling to Brittany to do the same. This story is similar to the *Life of Gwinear* by the Breton Anselm, and also borrows heavily from the *Life of Piran* (see Chapter 3). Orme suggests the author also had an earlier lost Cornish *Life of Sithney* as basis for his story. However he postulates that the saint's primary cult may have been in Brittany, as the Cornish village of Sithney is recorded in 1230 as *Merther-sitheny,* in other words a chapel, which would generally take its patron from another church site. It is unlikely that in this case Merther-sitheny meant 'The martyr Sithney' as all records seem to point to him living to a fine old age and that he was a 'monk and confessor', not a martyr. Other Breton traditions include that he was asked by God to be a patron of women but his attitude to them was somewhat bigoted, saying they would only pray to him for husbands and fine clothes. As a result he became the patron of mad dogs, and dogs were brought by their owners to drink from his well to be healed (Orme 2000: 236-7). He may have perhaps preferred the 'mad' women after all!

There is more than a little confusion between Sinnin and Senan. Whitaker places Sinnin as the patron of Sennan, near Land's End (1804 vol.1: 338), but this is contradicted by Baring-Gould who asserts that its saint was Senan, and identifies Sinnin with a pupil of Senan's called Setna. There is no surviving Life of Setna but he is spoken of in Senan's Life. Irish sources say Setna was a son of Erc and Magna, a sister of St. David[22]. Setna was a follower of Senan, a firm friend of his uncle David, and lived within his community at Inis Mór (Deer Island, County Clare). One day Setna and his fellow pupil Liberius castigated a woman for washing her child's clothes in the communal drinking fountain. Shortly afterwards, her child went

22 Irish traditions contradict the Welsh regarding St David and his mother St Non which say she remained celibate after his birth.

missing and she believed him drowned, and accused the pair of cursing him. Senan ordered the pair to do penance but Setna discovered the child on the beach alive and well and returned him to his mother, then fetched Liberius from the rock in the sea where he had been ordered to abandon him. After this he went to the abbey of Ciaran of Saighir and succeeded him there. This is perhaps why Sezni's *Life* by Albert Le Grand bore so much similarity to that of Piran, who is believed to be one and the same with Ciaran. Baring-Gould believes Setna followed Ciaran/Piran to Cornwall, and after establishing the church at Sithney, passed on to Brittany and founded his main cult centre of Guissény where the Breton *Life* says he died. It claims his relics wrought so many miracles the Irish reclaimed them, although this may indicate it is more likely he died in Ireland (1907 vol.4: 199-201).

In an attempt to give homes to the other companions, Whitaker places Helen at Helland, Elwin at St. Allen, and Maruan at Lamorran, although these claims do not hold up very well. Helena was only honoured at Helland from after the Reformation, its earlier dedication being to *Sinian* (Senan), and may only have been a mistake owing to the place name, which actually means 'ancient church site' (Orme 2000: 86). Helen is a name that occurs in multiple times and places in Celtic history and it is difficult to definitively place the Helen who travelled with Breaca at any church in the area. There is no record of St. Allen church ever being dedicated to Elwin, despite the similarity, its earliest dedication being to an *Alun*. The name may in fact be Saxon, translated as 'Beloved of all' (Drew 1824 vol.2: 28). Lamorran may have been dedicated to a female saint, Moren, as suggested by church records, or equally the place name may simply mean 'church upon the sea' (Drew 1824 vol2: 380). The name Maruan itself may have been misunderstood originally by Leland and actually referred to Mo-ruan ie. a diminutive form of Ruan/Rumon, who was, like Setna, another pupil of Senan's who came to Cornwall alongside the latter (Baring-Gould and Fisher 1907 vol. 4: 120) and will be discussed further in Chapter 7.

It is conjectured that a small band, minus Breaca, moved on from Cornwall to settle on the shores of the river Rance, near Dol, Brittany. The *History of the Church of Rheims* indicates that the siblings (although perhaps only brothers and sisters in Christ) Germanus, Fraclas, Helanus and Promptia (potentially Germoc, Thecla, Helen and Crewenna) migrated to the area. Alongside them was another Irish saint Achebran, also a disciple of Senan, whose name on his coming to Cornwall was transformed into Kevern. He is remembered at the village of St. Keverne at the Lizard Point, Cornwall and in Brittany alongside his aforementioned siblings who all have dedications in the same area (Baring-Gould and Fisher 1907 vol.1: 105-7).

Besides the story of the main band of travellers we have the curious addition of the journey of the seventeen-year-old virgin **Ia** mentioned in the *Life of Gwinear* and also referred to as *Hya.* She was born a nobleman's daughter and was a disciple of Barry, a companion of St. Patrick. It is known that a female disciple of Finbar i.e. Barry had a foundation at Cill Ia, although probably not at such an early age. Anselm tells us in the *Life of Gwinear* that as a new convert to Christianity she was eager to join Gwinear's mission but was late coming and missed the boat. Downhearted she slumped down in the sand and prayed that there could be some way in which she could follow the others, whilst idly prodding a fallen leaf with a stick. Her prayers were answered as the leaf enlarged to a size of a small one-man boat large enough to carry her on the water. She launched it into the waves, clambering atop, and finding a fast wind behind her was soon following the ships that were merely a dot on the horizon at this point. It has been surmised that the truth behind this story is in the similarity of the shape of Irish coracles to leaves[23]. She followed her countrymen across the sea but instead of landing on the Hayle side of the estuary she was blown to the headland of what is now the town of St. Ives. Her story is furthered in her own Life, now lost but seen by Leland. He recorded that a local lord Dinan[24], who controlled the land on that side of the estuary and presumably was a kinder ruler than Teudar, granted her land at Pendinas to build a church[25]. Leland also stated that she was not alone on her voyage but accompanied by Elwyn and others[26].

---

23 Another hypothesis is that this story was influenced by the journey of St. Bega, who travelled across the Irish Sea on a clump of grass to avoid an unwanted marriage to a prince of Norway (Baring-Gould and Fisher 1907 vol.3: 268).

24 Baring-Gould states that 'Dinan' was not a real name but simply a word meaning 'little fortress' (1907 vol.3: 268).

25 Orme questions the origin of Ia's cult as her church at St. Ives was originally only a chapel, as was her only other dedication at Troon in Camborne. It may be the case, as has been mooted about Sithney, that her cult originated in Brittany, in Plouyé (Parish of Ia)(2000: 144-5).

26 Leland's mention that Ia was not alone on her voyage is taken by Whitaker to mean that the company came simultaneously in two boats, one with Breaca landing on the east shore and one with Ia landing on the west (1804 vol.2: 2).

Amongst Ia's companions may have been Euny and Erc, whom William of Worcester believed to be her brothers. **Erc** (or *Ergh*)'s church can be found near to St. Ives in the parish of St. Erth (the eventual anglicised form of his name) with an additional chapel also in the parish. The only other information from William of Worcester about Erc was that he was a bishop and his feast day was the 31st October. There are several possibilities as to the identity of this Erc. He is often associated with Erc of Slane, a bishop and convert of Patrick.

This Erc began life as the son of Degain, a judge of a pagan king, Laoghaire. It is told that on 31st October 455, at the festival of Samhain, St. Patrick lit a bonfire on the hill of Slane. This displeased the King who had ordered every fire in the country to be extinguished that night. He ordered the person responsible to be put to death. Laoghaire's druids advised that they travel to Slane and request his presence, but that they receive him seated so as to show him no respect. Patrick responded to the king's summons and found all the men seated except for one, Erc, who rose at Patrick's words, saying they illuminated his soul. Even the king was eventually won over and Patrick was allowed to stay and preach. Erc was baptised at the behest of Patrick and ten years later consecrated bishop. Slane became his monastic centre and as the son of a man of the law, helped Patrick in the judgment of cases that came before him. These details come from the *Life of St Patrick* and we do not have a *Life* of Erc himself to tell us when or if he came to Cornwall. The Irish annals date his death at 512 on the 2nd November, although the Cornish were said to hold that it was two days earlier, which was the same date as his conversion. There are several Irish Ercs and it is possible that this Erc was another pupil of Senan's. Orme thinks that it is even possible he may have been a local born Cornish saint that was later given Irish origins, as was popular in the Middle Ages (2000: 117).

Right: St. Ia: This plucky young princess, Ia, followed her fellows across the Irish Sea on a miraculously large leaf, landing and settling at the site of the modern town of St. Ives. Acrylic on canvas board (16in x 20in).

Euny is identified in an Irish martyrology with Eogain, son of Erc, Bishop of Slane rather than brother; although these terms were perhaps used only in a spiritual sense. Eogain is spoken of in the *Life* of St. Tigernach, his friend and companion. The *Life* tells how the pair were sold into slavery but eventually regained their liberty and set up a church together at Clones, Ireland, before Eogain moved on to become Bishop of Ardstraw. His deeds include warning a pagan chieftain, Amalghaid, against baptising his new spear with the blood of an innocent child, as was their custom. The chieftain ignored Eogain and died within a few days, presumably as a result. Eogain also managed to break into a dun (a Dark Age hill fort) that had been besieged by pirates, baptise the hundred or so inhabitants, and sneak them out of the siege by cloaking them in a fog!

There is no other information about Euny's Irish origins and we have only William of Worcester's word that Euny and Erc were relations of Ia. His cult in Cornwall was quite prolific and may well point to him being a local saint. Unlike Erc's single foundation there, Euny had at least five cult sites, including a joint dedication at the church of Crowan and a chapel and well in Sancreed that reportedly had healing powers. His original cult centre was likely to have been Lelant, which is on the banks of the Hayle, the same side as St. Ives, and is said to be where Euny is buried (Orme 2000: 119-20). The name of the place however means 'church site of Anta' and many have speculated that this Anta was the original inhabitant of the site, a hermit whom Gwinear and company observed on their landing.

Although the various accounts suggest Gwinear and company brought Christianity to an otherwise pagan territory, the presence of the hermit Anta and the 'good Christian' Conuria in the locality leads us to speculate on whether this band of Irish settlers really were the first bringers of the faith or not. Besides these inhabitants there is suggestion that this mission was later than the arrivals of Senan, who earned the discipleship of many other saints, and Piran, another contemporary who is claimed to be the founder of the oldest church in Cornwall.

Chapter 3

Cornwall's Patron Saint - Piran, Petroc, or Michael?

Ask any Cornish folk who the patron saint of their county is and you may get one of at least three different answers. Whilst other British counties generally do not claim a patron saint, the somewhat archaic perception of Cornwall as a separate Celtic 'country' endures and therefore so does the desire to name a national patron. In modern times the most common answer is likely to be Piran, potentially due to the fairly recent association of the Cornish flag with this saint. He was certainly Cornwall's most popular saint amongst the laity around the eighteenth and nineteenth centuries, due to the widespread folk legend that cast him as the patron of tinners, tin being at one time one of Cornwall's largest industries. In earlier centuries the answer would most likely have been Michael the Archangel, despite not being a 'local' saint; just as the similarly depicted Syrian saint, George, is the patron of the English. He is of course patron of one of Cornwall's most recognisable landmarks, St. Michael's Mount, and a host of other high places dedicated to the Archangel that stretch into Devon, Somerset, and beyond. Besides these two is also Petroc, whom we could consider to be the most prolific of Cornwall's saints, having eight cult centres in Cornwall and more in neighbouring counties. All three are considered patrons of Cornwall, but does any have a greater claim than the others?

Cult Centres and Origins

Our first candidate, Piran, has three cult centres in Cornwall, the oldest thought to be at Perranzabuloe which is situated near the coast a little way south from Newquay. It lies slightly inland from

Perranporth, presumably the beach at which Piran landed on his arrival from Ireland.[27] Here we have another saint whose origins may have been native to Cornwall but the details of which were forgotten by the later Middle Ages and replaced, as seemed to be the fashion, with a tale of Irish beginnings.

Historians disagree on the true birthplace and personage of Piran. A commonly held view is that he was identical with the Irish saint Ciarán of Saighir.[28] Although Leland describes him as the 'disciple of Patrick' the date of his birth suggests he preceded Patrick. Whitaker aims to explain this anachronism by saying that Piran/Ciarán was one of four clergymen who preached in Ireland prior to Patrick's coming in the mid-fifth century but unlike the other three, he showed subjection to Patrick after his arrival and therefore became known as a 'disciple of Patrick' (1804 vol.2: 5-7).[29] The Irish biography states he became a hermit and died in Ireland while the British adaptation sees his monastery grow in size and visitorship, and in order to find solitude he removes himself to Cornwall. Although the original *Life of Ciarán* does not mention Cornwall it does say he went abroad from Ireland for thirty years which could account for his coming.

Right: St Michael: Here the Archangel Michael is pictured over the Mount which is now dedicated to him, a towering vision revealed to the fishermen below. His appearance is somewhat inspired by the Greek solar deity Apollo, another patron of hilltop sun-stations. Acrylic on canvas board (16in x 20in).

---

27 Piran's other cult centres were at Perranarworthal and Perranuthnoe, later additions in the 13th and 14th centuries originating from the cult at Perranzabuloe. Perranarworthal is said to mean 'Perran on the noted river' whilst Perranuthnoe means 'Little Perran' and Perranzabuloe means 'Perran in the Sands' (Hunt 1903: 273). A medieval chapel and well at Trevethy, near Tintagel have been attributed to St. Piran but the proximity to the Kieve of St Nectan has called into question their original dedication (Orme 2000: 222).

28 This view may be due to a twelfth century manuscript which adapts the *Life of Ciarán* and adds in the names of his parents and a voyage to Cornwall where it states he died and was buried, and add to this the fact that *p* in Brittonic often translated to *c* in the Irish language. Leland saw the adaptation and records that Piran was also known as Kyeran (Orme 2000: 221).

29 Whitaker places him in the company of Breaca and Sinnin which would be very improbable if we take his birth to be 352 and Breaca's mission from Ireland to Cornwall to be circa 460 (1804 vol.2: 7).

Other scholars such as Doble regard Piran as having Welsh origins and that he attended the school of Cadoc at Llancarfan. His presence in the area is somewhat supported by the mention by Gerald of Wales in the twelfth century of a now lost chapel in Cardiff dedicated to St. Piran.

The cult of Petroc was far more widespread, with seven or eight dedications in Cornwall and as many as seventeen in Devon with others as far afield as Wales, Brittany and Winchester.[30] The earliest surviving *Life of Petroc* we have dates to the eleventh century, and is most likely Cornish from the priory at Bodmin. This gives Petroc's origins as Welsh, and were expanded upon in a twelfth century Life written at Bodmin, to give us Glywys as his father and Cadoc as his nephew, in whose Life he also appears. Petroc was a prince who renounced his birthright and entered holy orders instead, travelling to Ireland with companions to live in a monastery for the next twenty years. Alternately, a fifteenth-century Welsh source states Petroc to be the son of a Cornish king, and even that he was a warrior! The poem claimed he was one of the few knights to escape King Arthur's last battle at Camlan before entering the Church. One of his Welsh churches, Llanbedrog, even claimed to hold his famed spear![31]

Saint Michael is of course the Archangel of the Bible and therefore canonical and international, separating him from the British saints we have encountered so far. Cornwall's most famous landmark bears his name, as do many other church sites in Cornwall and the South West. Besides Saint Michael's Mount a great many other sites are dedicated to the Archangel in Cornwall,

---

30 Petroc's Cornish churches include his original cult centre of Padstow and the neighbouring parishes of Little Petherick and Trebetherick, Bodmin Minster and Priory, and the parish churches of Bodmin, Egloshayle and Trevalga, with the late addition of Egloskerry in 1733. There is another chapel in Padstow that is also probably dedicated to Petroc under the appellation *Pedyr*. Petroc's medieval church sites in Devon include Clannaborough, Cotleigh, Exeter, Farringdon, Harpford, Hollacombe, Lydford, Newton St Petrock, Petrockstow, South Brent, Tormohun, West Anstey, with the possible additions West Worlington and Dunkeswell. More were added in more recent times. The church at Timberscombe in Somerset is also dedicated to him (Orme 2000: 214-9).

31 The Welsh poem was written by a man of the parish of Verwick in Cardigan, where the church of Landpedrog stood, as a prayer to Petroc to save the village from encroaching sand dunes. It shows how vastly different the Welsh and Cornish traditions were concerning Petroc. A contemporary manuscript calls him Pedrog Splintered-Spear, one of the three just knights of King Arthur's court, and it is this spear that Llanbedrog in Gwynedd claimed to house and accepted cash offerings for (Orme 2000: 218-9).

many of them being found on high ground. It has been postulated that this is because of their proximity to heaven or perhaps that these St. Michael churches represent suppression of the old pagan Britons who had previously used such sites, possibly for worship. In Christian cosmology, Michael's body is the sun, which banishes the demonic forces to the Underworld at these notable hill sites (Pennick 1996: 83). This is one interpretation of the famous motif of Michael slaying a dragon, the dragon representing the old religion and being conquered by the mighty sword of Christianity. Another theory is that Michael's nature and appearance evolved from pre-Christian solar deities such as Apollo and Mithras, 'the unconquerable sun', as well as Hermes, who shares Michael's role as psychopomp – a guide for the souls of the dead (Hill 1916: 143-5) These sites have solar significance, often aligning with the May day sunrise as well as serving as mystical entrances to the Underworld. It is therefore suggested that Michael replaced the pagan deities as master of these sun stations using similar imagery to 'ease people into the new religion' as was commonly the way with Christianity in the early centuries, its holidays often coinciding with older pagan festivals.

Peregrination

According to legend, Piran was born in Ireland to wealthy parents Domuel and Wingela. During his early life he became a Christian and disciple of the great Saint Patrick. He travelled to Rome where he tarried for twenty years, learning the scriptures and earning the respect of the Pope before returning home to preach to his countrymen. However not all of them were happy to receive him and a band of heathen Irish tied him to a millstone and toppled him over a cliff to drown him. Little did they expect the power of God to overcome this wicked deed and as soon as that millstone hit the water it floated and the crowd watching from the clifftop were all instantly converted. The millstone bobbed across the Irish sea and ended up in Cornwall at the place now known as Perranporth. Piran was greeted by folk who were much more welcoming and loved his new home. He was joined later on by more of his converts including his mother Wingela and they built his church at Perranzabuloe, said to be the oldest foundation in Cornwall, where he lived and died.

Above: St. Piran: The hardy Irish saint Piran stands beside the millstone that carried him to Cornwall and in front of the St. Piran's cross in the dunes of Perranporth, where the yearly celebrations of his feast day are held. Acrylic on canvas (20in x 24in).

Unlike Piran who came after being cast out, Petroc set sail for Cornwall on a mission of conversion although the initial greeting he received was none too friendly. On their arrival, Petroc and his devout followers asked some harvesters where they could find water but the stubborn locals refused to tell, so Petroc drove his staff into the ground to make a spring for himself. The place where Petroc and his companions had landed was the estuary at modern day Padstow, then known as Landuvethnoc, after a bishop who lived there called Wethenoc. The author of the first *Life* must have known of this and explains it by neatly having Wethenoc happily hand over his living quarters to Petroc in return for naming the place after him when he was gone (E. Rees 2001: 139). He thanked the bishop kindly and took up residence there, and from that day Petroc and his followers tended to that part of the country for thirty years. St. Samson was also supposedly present in this region at this time but was not happy about Petroc's arrival and deciding that the area was not big enough for the both of them, moved on to found his own monastery elsewhere. Petroc's stay in Padstow only ended because, he allegedly prophesied the end to a rainy season and was disproved the next day when it poured once more. Subsequently, he felt he had no choice but to leave in embarrassment!

St. Michael's Mount is so named because, according to local legend, the Archangel appeared to fishermen above the Mount around the year 495.[32] This story is likely to have been influenced by a similar apparition of Michael at Monte Gargano in Italy in 490 when the Archangel instructed the bishop to create a place of worship there. However his cult did not reach England until around the eight century and Cornwall itself until the eleventh with the coming of the Normans. The monastery of Mont-Saint-Michel in Normandy, where another vision of Michael had occurred in the eighth century, lent its support to William the Conqueror and was rewarded with the site of the Cornish Mount. Here they built, or possibly rebuilt, a monastery which remained under their rule until the time of Henry V (Orme 2000: 192-5).

Although the feast day of Saint Michael is 29th September (Michaelmas), the more commonly celebrated day in Cornwall is May 8th, the date of his apparition in the county, incidentally the same date as his appearance at Mount Gargano. The perennially popular folk festival, the Furry Dance, held in Helston every year on May 8th is said to owe its origins to Saint Michael. Some say this peculiarly Cornish festival which dates back to the Middle Ages commemorates the defeat of the Devil, in the form of a dragon, in a mid-air battle with Saint Michael. Other variations include a fight between the pair commencing over Mont Saint-Michel during which Michael retreated to the Cornish Mount, knowing his adversary could not follow him across water. In a rage, Satan tore the lid from the mouth of Hell and flung it across the channel, the landing place being the centre of the town whose name

---

32 Carew, visiting the Mount at the beginning of the seventeenth century, reported that its name in Cornish was *Clara Clowse in Cowse* (altnerative Carrek Los y'n Cos), translated as 'Hoary (Grey) Rock in the Wood', a vestige of ancient timeswhen the bay had been a forest.

derived from this “Hell-stone”[33] (Nance, 1951: 15).

Miracles

Piran's miracles are well documented. He fed ten Irish kings and their armies for ten days on just three cows! He is also said to have brought hunting dogs and warriors back to life. The most famous story about him, recorded in Hunt's nineteenth-century book of West Country legends, regards his discovering of tin. In his little cell in the sands he built himself a fireplace. Above this he had placed a massive slab of black rock. After some time the rock got very hot, and started to produce a silvery-white liquid, which Piran noted and showed to his friend Saint Chiwidden. Together they showed the local people how to find the correct rocks and extract the tin. This is how he became the patron of tinners in the county and allegedly why the flag of Cornwall is a white cross on a black background, representing the white metal and the black ore (Hunt 1903: 274-5). It should be pointed out that tin mining had been in operation in Cornwall for centuries before the time of Saint Piran and traded during the occupation of the Romans in Britain. We can speculate that at best Piran reminded the native Cornish of the process of extraction after a lapse in production following Roman withdrawal.

Petroc’s journeys were even more miraculous than Piran’s voyage on the millstone. After thirty years in Cornwall, he went travelling abroad to Rome and Jerusalem on holy pilgrimage. He even went as far afield as India where it was said a magical silver bowl appeared to him, which he stepped on and was taken to a tiny island which he made his home for seven years. Other feats accomplished on his journey include taking a splinter from a dragon's eye, and befriending a wolf who became his companion and is sometimes depicted by his side.

Petroc was told by an angel to return specifically because Cornwall needed him. Immediately on his return, Petroc was called to banish a serpent. The local king Tewdrig had a tank of snakes and serpents which he had been using to put criminals to death. After Tewdrig's son took over he put a stop to this barbaric practice and having no more thieves to feast on, the creatures turned on each other until one came out victorious growing to such a massive size that it was able to get out and terrorize the local farms. On

33 The less fantastical origin for the town name is from its medieval Cornish name 'Hellys', meaning 'old court' and 'ton', a Saxon suffix for 'manor'.

hearing about this, Petroc went with his old friends Samson and Wethnoc and bound the beast's mouth and chasing it into the sea. Similar dragon-slaying stories are told in the *Life* of Samson.

Besides converting the heathen Tewdrig, Petroc's words persuaded another king, Constantine, to give up his wicked ways. The story goes that after returning to Cornwall, Petroc and some companions made their home in Little Petherick. Nearby, King Constantine was out hunting deer. A stag he was chasing came to shelter at Petroc's cell. Upon confronting Petroc and hearing what he had to say, the chieftain and his whole band of warriors were converted to Christianity. Although a fairly old man at the time of his conversion, Constantine apparently gave up his throne and entered Holy Orders. The nearby St. Constantine's Bay was probably named after this King-turned-holy man.

There is not much that is more miraculous than the divine appearance of an Archangel decreeing the construction of a monastery, albeit perhaps a story borrowed from across the channel. Despite separation from the mother house of Mont Saint-Michel in the late fourteenth century, pilgrimage to the St. Michael's Mount continued up until the Reformation, with many seeking the legendary 'Chair of St. Michael', a precariously placed rock slab said to be the site of the Archangel's appearance. Many of the legends attached to the Mount seem to have been transferred from Mont Saint-Michel after the break from Normandy and appropriated by the English, such as the motif of an appearance of Michael to the local bishop with the request of building his church. In this way Saint Michael was absorbed into the Cornish culture and taken on as their own patron in the Middle Ages. Other stories featuring the Mount and Saint Michael abound, including one which ties in with the other legends that state that the island was built by giants. The tale of 'Saint Michael and the Conger' is a quaint story of how Michael takes on the role of 'giant slayer', previously held by Jack (Harris 1906: 15-17).[34]

---

34 'Saint Michael and the Conger' written in the early twentieth century offers an alternative explanation to how The Mount got its name. Here Michael is portrayed as much more of a down-to-earth saint, certainly not with the wings of an archangel! Landing upon the island he discovers a great many 'Keep Out' signs, particularly directed at saints, posted by the inhabitant of the Mount, a giant who Michael could hear snoring from the Mount's summit. When a giant conger eel surfaces, arching up into the air, Michael takes the opportunity to scale it to reach the summit using his spurs where he beheads the giant. A church miraculously springs up which Michael dedicates to

Patronage

Piran's Oratory at Perranzabuloe survives to this day, although its ruins are now buried in sand. It was built around the sixth century and remained in use right up until the sixteenth, when the windblown sands overtook it. The draining of a nearby lake may have been to blame for the sand's incursion which had previously protected the Oratory from being overtaken. An eighteenth century excavation unveiled many bodies buried two feet beneath the floor including a man of a reported height of 7'5 who was headless, which corresponds to the story of Piran's head being removed to the daughter church of St. Agnes (Mildren 1989: 20-2).

The same fate as Piran's Oratory awaited Piran's church which had been an important minister centre in the eleventh century. By the nineteenth century it had to be abandoned and relocated to its present position. Not long after, in 1835, the Oratory was rediscovered and excavated but by 1910 it was under threat again and enclosed in a building of concrete and perspex for its protection and eventually allowed to be taken by the sands once again.

The minster church, which was by 1281 demoted to a parish church, retained the relics of Piran which were brought out annually and taken in procession about the parish. These included a reliquary containing Piran's head, and one containing his bowl, his staff, his cross, and a copper bell (Orme 2000: 221). This tradition continued for several centuries but the relics are not known to have survived the Reformation. St. Piran's Day celebrations were revived in the eighteenth century by tinners who had taken Piran for their patron and popularised the legend that Piran was the discoverer of tin. The celebrations took place on the anniversary of his death, March 5th and involved the Perraners, a nickname for tinners, downing tools and making much revelry.

Right: St. Petroc: A saint fond of nature, Petroc stands besides the stag he sheltered from King Constantine. Petroc saved the life of the stag and converted the king – all in a day's work! Acrylic on canvas (16in x 24in).

---

himself! It also mentions how he became the patron saint of Cornwall after encountering and defeating the Devil at Helston (Harris 1906: 15-17).

The saying 'drunk as a Perraner' originated from this time. The marking of St. Piran's Day as a 'national' holiday grew increasingly popular in the twentieth-century across the whole county and included a procession across the sands at Perranporth, bearing Cornish flags, which continues to this day.

The author of the second *Life of Petroc* states that the saint died and was buried at Padstow. If this is the case then his relics would have been removed to another of his centres, Bodmin, when the northern coast was laid waste by Vikings in the late tenth century. Bodmin had become an Augustine monastery in c.1124 and kept the relics up until the Reformation except for a brief period when they were stolen by one of the canons and taken to Brittany. They were recovered, although King Henry II permitted the abbey of Saint Meen, where they had been taken, to retain four bones. Relics of Petroc abound, at Exeter Cathedral, at Waltham Abbey, Glastonbury Abbey, and more. Bodmin retains the reliquary that was said to have housed the saint's head, the box now empty.

Petroc's integration into the English church and the spread of his cult is undoubted, relics perhaps being taken further afield in the interests of promoting integration with the Anglo-Saxons. His importance is shown in that, besides Piran and Neot, he is the only Cornish saint to feature in John of Tynemouth's important record of British saints *Nova Legenda Anglie.* Nicholas Roscarrock noted that, similarly to Piran, processions from Petroc's main cult sites of Bodmin, Padstow and Little Petherick went about on the saint's feast day, the 4th June, in the pre-Reformation period (Orme 2000: 216-8). Besides his Cornish sites, the sacred well of his Welsh church of Llanbedrog drew pilgrims seeking cures for gangrene and other ailments, and was used to divine for the culprit in cases of thievery, by floating a piece of bread on its surface and watching to see if it sank when the suspect's name was uttered (Baring-Gould and Fisher 1907 vol.4: 102).

The significant Cornish dedications to St. Michael fall on what has become famously known as 'The St. Michael leyline', an almost perfect straight line or 'corridor of incidence' that runs from the tip of Cornwall right through Great Britain following the course of the May day sunrise, on the important Celtic fire festival of Beltane. In their book *'The Sun and the Serpent'*, earth-energy investigators Hamish Miller and Paul Broadhurst detailed the churches, wells, stone circles and monuments, and general points of interest that fell on this line, many of which were dedicated to Saint Michael or his dragon-slaying earthly counterpart Saint George, and also a great number to Saint Mary (1989: 32-4).[35]

In Cornwall we find Roche Rock, an imposing and windswept outcrop of granite near St. Austell which houses a chapel to St. Michael built in 1409 that served as a hermitage throughout the ages.[36] Along this line we also find the churches of St. Michael Penkevil and Perranuthnoe, interestingly the latter a joint dedication to Michael and Saint Piran. In addition are Michaelstow and a priory of monks at Lamanna, the origin of which is as old as the one at the Mount. There also exists the remains of a St. Michael chapel on Roughtor, one of the highest spots in the county. Barely over the border in Devon is the hilltop church of St. Michael *de Rupe* ('of the rock') at Brentor, previously an Iron Age hillfort. It was built around 1130 and legend has it that the church was originally sited at the base of the tor but that overnight the Devil moved its foundation to the top. At the intervention of Saint Michael, the Devil was defeated but the church remained in its lofty position and dedicated to the archangel. St. Michael was said to have scared off the Devil by hurling a massive boulder, which still lies at the base of the tor to this day.

If we continue to look beyond Cornwall's borders more of these hilltop churches can be found at Burrow Mump and Glastonbury Tor in Somerset, both dedicated to Saint Michael. In Powys, Wales, however, rather than dedications on high places we find four St. Michael churches encircling one – the hill of Radnor Forest. The local legend was that the last dragon of Wales was confined beneath the hill and the churches of Llanfihangel Cefnllys, Llanfihangel

---

35 Miller and Broadhurst reported the finds of their dowsing expedition which took them the breadth of the country through many notable and 'sacred' sites. Particular points of interest were marked by what they call a 'node', a place where the energy flows traced by the dowsers converge and bury into the ground then reappear and continue onward. After tracing the first line which they had dubbed 'Michael' they discovered a separate line that ran almost parallel, sometimes weaving and crossing it. This they dubbed 'Mary'. Characteristically the sites along 'Michael' were of a more solar, masculine quality and comprised of many high places, beacons and earthworks; the line itself being a lot straighter than 'Mary' which was more sinuous and contained sites of a more watery quality such as holy wells which they interpreted as feminine.

36 Whilst the chapel on Roche Rock is dedicated to St. Michael, the village church of Roche's patron saint is Gonand (possibly Conan, Gundred or Gonnet). The Rock was used as a hermitage for the holy (Conan, one of Cornwall's first Bishops was said to have been a hermit here), and the sick. Gundred was the daughter of a leper who had been placed in a cell on the Rock for the health of the parishioners. She fetched food for her father and water from the nearby well which became named after her (James 1993: 55).

Rhydithon, Llanfihangel Nantmelan, and Llanfihangel Cascob were built in a ring around it to contain it. It is said if any of the churches are ever destroyed, the dragon will be free to wreak havoc on the countryside once more.

***

So can the 'true' patron of Cornwall be decided upon from their number of churches, their heavenly ranking, or how ancient of days they are? It could be argued that as Michael's dedications extend right the way across the country he could be considered a 'wholly English' saint rather than just of Cornwall. Whilst it is quite possible Piran at least may have really been a native Cornishman, curiously it is not claimed that any of the three have Cornish origins. On one hand Petroc was said to have arrived by choice whereas Piran did not, but Piran's coming could perhaps be described as fate and God's will. The British claim the Irishman never again left his new heartland after his miraculous journey to Cornwall. Petroc's influence on the Celtic church in Cornwall was considerable, founding eight churches, including two of its most important, Bodmin and Padstow; yet an even greater number of his foundations are to be found in Devon and beyond. Devon adopted a flag in 2006 named 'St. Petroc's flag', similar to Cornwall's flag of St. Piran but featuring a white cross on a green background, making him arguably more Devon's patron saint. However Cornwall claimed his relics and was regarded as their proper home. The procession on St Piran's Day is Cornwall at its most patriotic but St. Michael's Mount draws in pilgrims and tourists all year round. The more romantically inclined, such as Wellesley Tudor Pole, founder of the Chalice Well Trust in Glastonbury, envisioned the trail of dedications to the Archangel in Cornwall – Saint Michael's Way – to be the herald for the coming again of Christ, returning to walk again on the turf of the New Jerusalem as he did "in ancient times" on his way to Avalon (1951:24-5).

All three of these saints have at some point in history been Cornwall's most prominent saint. There is no definitive means of providing the answer; perhaps it is one that can only be found in the hearts of the Cornish...

Chapter 4

Glastonbury
An Accumulation of Saints

Next we turn our attention to the small, yet widely famed, town of Glastonbury in Somerset. It is likely the reader will know of it and be able to associate an image with the town today, whether it be of the iconic Tor topped with the tower of St. Michael, the sprawling Abbey ruins, the bustling plethora of New Age shops, or the yearly music festival. Although a lot of focus on the town has grown out of the New Age phenomenon of the last 50 years, its history is long and its legends stretch back even further. To answer "Why this particular place?" may be a near-impossible task, and to attempt to find a reason for the attraction of so many myths to the place and unravel the history from the legend may be fruitless and potentially missing the point. What we do know is the town seamlessly blends the elements of Arthurian lore and Glastonbury-as-Avalon, with the possibility of visits by Jesus and Joseph of Arimathea and an abundance of other saints, alongside pagan Goddess worship and earth spirituality; and if we accept we cannot fully separate these elements from each other we can understand its spirituality a little better.

As esoteric writer Dion Fortune put it, "There are many Glastonburys, and though her walls have never been cast down, like the walls of Troy, her spirit has hidden levels, depth below depth, like the rocks of a mountain range, and in different places these come to the surface" (2000: 35). This is a huge topic in itself, enough to fill several books and, of course, we are primarily concerned with the saints of this place, specifically how some of the more internationally well-known saints like the Irish Patrick and Brigid, and biblical Michael and Joseph of Arimathea came to be associated with the town of Glastonbury. Besides these there are other saints more specific to the region such as Dunstan, as well as other south-western names such as Kea, Rumon, and Neot who may have been educated here, and the bones of others that may have been translated to Glastonbury after their deaths.

One potential reason for the visits of such illustrious saints may be Glastonbury's claim as the site of the oldest church in Britain. The first Archbishop of Canterbury, Augustine, is credited with officially founding the English Church when he was sent on a mission from Rome in the year 596. However, much is made of the theory that earlier missions saw Christianity come to these isles in the very early days of the Christian church led by Simon Zelotes, Aristobulus, Joseph of Arimathea, and Saint Paul. English monk Bede, writing one hundred years later, told how the British bishops at the council called by Augustine rejected his terms and refused to submit to Rome, preferring to keep to the ways that we would identify in modern times as 'Celtic Christianity' (although a far from unified Church at the time).[37] It is claimed by many that Joseph of Arimathea, whom we shall come back to later, built the first wattle church at Glastonbury under instruction from Saint Gabriel, some time shortly after Christ's death and resurrection. British historian and saint himself, Gildas, who retired to and died at Glastonbury in 570, said that "as we know" Britain received the teachings of Christ in the reign of Tiberius Caesar, i.e. by 37 CE, pointing to an accepted legend of an early visit by a follower of Jesus (Lewis 1925: 2). Later additions to the work of twelfth century Glastonbury historian William of Malmesbury claim that Joseph and his company of eleven men were sent on a mission by Saint Philip the Apostle and on their arrival were granted a measure of land known as the 'Twelve Hides' of Glastonbury by the King Arviragus, and were exempt from paying tax. Here they stayed until their eventual deaths upon which the church was reclaimed by nature (Lewis 1925: 4).

---

37 R. W. Morgan, an upholder of the claim that Saint Paul visited Britain, stresses the apostolic nature, character and origin of the British church as opposed to a Roman one, going as far as to claim it to be older than the Church in Rome, and being administered to directly by the followers of Christ after the Resurrection. He states of the British "How came they, on their first meeting with the missionary of the Bishop of Rome, to proclaim with one voice 'We have nothing to do with Rome; we know nothing of the Bishop of Rome in his new character of the Pope; we are the British Church, the Archbishop of which is accountable to God alone, having no superior on earth'" (1938: 179-80). Although the unanimity of 'the British Church' is probably exaggerated here, it is likely that Celtic Christians did have their own views and heritage in their own right, separate from Rome.

Above: St. Patrick: An icon of the world-famous Irish saint, Patrick, who is said to have come to Glastonbury as its first abbot. Acrylic and gold leaf on wood (11.5in x 9.5in).

Although the physical church had decayed, legend has the 'first Christian king of Britain', Lucius, writing to Pope Eleutherius asking for missionaries, around one hundred years after the coming of Joseph. The tale was recounted by Bede, and later retold by Geoffrey of Monmouth and William of Malmesbury, who added more details telling of the missionaries Phagan and Deruvian (latinisations of their earlier recorded names Fagan and Dyfan) and how they led another group of twelve to resurrect and rebuild the Old Church in memory of the first twelve.[38] The story is neatly concluded with successive groups of twelve inhabiting the cells surrounding the church right up to the coming of Saint Patrick who is credited with becoming their first Abbot.

Saint **Patrick** is a figure of enormous symbolic significance and legendary status, being associated with the very character of Ireland itself as its patron saint and reportedly its first bishop. Like Glastonbury itself, evidence about the historical Patrick is extremely elusive and it is theorised that at least two different Patricks existed, some saying as many as five, that were conflated into one in the telling of how Ireland was converted.[39] Evidence for his being at

---

38 Historical evidence of a real king named Lucius is lacking although he is mentioned by several medieval writers. Geoffrey of Monmouth states that the story of Lucius and the coming of Fagan and Dyfan was recorded by Gildas although this chronicle was lost (Lewis 1925: 10). Bede, Geoffrey and William all agree on Lucius sending for missionaries and asking for baptism of his own free will although it is claimed that the story may be a later claim to 'early Christianity' by the English and that the basis for Bede's account, the *Liber Pontificalis* may be talking about an entirely different king and kingdom in Syria.

39 Rev. Baring-Gould wrote at length about the different Patricks that may have been absorbed into, and expanded the legend of, the figure of Saint Patrick. He draws the conclusion that the bishop initially sent to minister to the Irish by Pope Celestine I in 431 can be identified as Palladius who failed in his mission, dying in 432. He surmises that the Patrick active in Ireland from 432 was the Patrick from the Welsh tradition known as Mawon or Magonius, whose death is given as 457 and this may have been the 'Great Patrick', the apostle to the Irish. He believes it to be more likely that this honour belongs to Patrick MacCalpurn, the author of the *Confession* whose writings tell of how he was sold into slavery in Ireland at the age of sixteen, eventually escaping and returning to his family and later going back to Ireland as archapostle after a prompt from an inner voice, and dying in 493. Patrick Magonius may have studied with Germanus of Auxerre and been sent for commission by Celestine to go to Ireland in 432 but this likely arises from confusion with Palladius and yet another Patrick, disciple of Germanus, Bishop of Man. Desire by chroniclers to conflate these men into one prompted anachronisms, primarily the gap between Celestine's mission and the death of Patrick MacCalpurn in 493, solved by having his life equal the length of Moses' 120 years (Baring-Gould and Fisher 1907 vol.4: 54-69).

Glastonbury is even rarer and localised; there is no mention in any Irish source of his coming. The *Confession,* a piece attributed to the hand of Patrick himself tells how he was sold into slavery at the age of sixteen and was in Ireland six years before his escape and eventual return as bishop and apostle. It defends his practices against charges of impropriety and accepting gifts in return for his ministering although strangely does not validate his mission by mentioning whose authority he was sent on. These are the details that may have been conflated from other sources.

William of Malmesbury writes that Patrick was taken into the company of St. Germanus and sent to Pope Celestine to preach to the Irish in 425 CE. He adds that in later years he returned to Britain living out his last days at Glastonbury and was buried in the Old Church (Lewis 1925: 14). He tells how Patrick came upon twelve hermits, successors of the original twelve, and unwillingly (as he felt unworthy) agreed to lead them. He describes how, in a ruined oratory atop Glastonbury Tor, Patrick discovers the Acts and Deeds of Phagan and Deruvian that tell of how they built the chapel to St. Michael (Lewis 1925: 17). Additional information in William's *Antiquities of Glastonbury* about the great fire that destroyed the original church in 1184 proves interpolation by other hands after William's death, bringing into question the authenticity of the entire document. As we will see, efforts were made by the monks to bring in revenue after the fire, which possibly included their discovery of the 'graves' of King Arthur and Guinevere. However this particular tradition regarding Patrick may not have been a fabrication of William's or the later monks' as the Bosworth Psalter, a text of around 150 years older than William, makes mention of 'Patrick the Elder' at Glastonbury (Gasquet, Bishop and St. Toke 1908: 21). Whether Patrick's presence there was invented or not, he became intrinsically linked to the Abbey and drew in great numbers of Irish pilgrims, and reportedly saints, to see his relics that were said to be there. The neighbouring area called Beckery was populated by Irish settlers and the name was thought to mean 'Little Ireland' (Lewis 1925: 15).[40]

The Abbey itself houses a sixteenth century Chapel of St. Patrick which served as an almshouse chapel, and was restored in

---

40 Glastonbury certainly had Irish settlers from at least the ninth century as evidenced in the *Life* of St Dunstan which tells of his Irish teachers, and also in tenth century charters referring to Beckery as 'Little Ireland', its etymology possibly coming from the Old Irish *Becc-Eriu* although more probably from the Old English *Beocere* - 'beekeeper's island' (Rahtz 1993: 150).

recent years to give it a medieval character once again.

William of Malmesbury expands upon his Patrick legend by having another Irish saint and disciple of Saint Patrick, Saint **Benignus**, succeed him as abbot of Glastonbury on his death. Benignus, he tells us, was buried in the outlying village of Meare and later translated to the Abbey. The body of a hermit named Beon was certainly moved to the Abbey in 1091; whether he was Benignus of Armagh is speculation. His tomb bore an engraving which was said to have been lifted from his original grave - “In this tomb Father Beonna's bones are placed, who was the father of the monks here in ancient times. He was in all probability, Patrick's servant for a long time. So say the Hibernians, and they call him 'Beonna'”[41]. This suggests veneration amongst the Irish pilgrims in the vicinity and perhaps even an Irish origin for Beon; but whether the association with Benignus of Armagh stemmed from these devotees or from the monks of the Abbey we do not know. Here we see a pattern beginning to form of the 'accumulation' of saints to Glastonbury, even before the fire of 1184. A church was built and dedicated to Benignus on the site of Beon's final resting place, which today has become St. Benedict's. It has links with the church on the site of the original grave in Meare, which is dedicated to St. Mary.

William continues to tell us of the coming of Saint **Brigid** (or Bride) in the time of the reign of Benignus at Glastonbury and following in the footsteps of Patrick whom she admired. Saint Brigid's stay in Glastonbury was a relatively short one but the story is one that has been recounted many times. A hugely popular figure in Ireland, and considered one of the country's three patron saints; she was revered further afield also and Glastonbury is proud to have hosted her, even for a short time. The saint is also believed by some to have been syncretized with the pre-Christian Celtic goddess Brighid, taking on some of the characteristics of the goddess. This makes her presence here in Glastonbury doubly popular as modern Goddess-worshippers associate it with the presence of the Sacred Feminine in the landscape of Glastonbury.

Distinctions between the goddess, the legends of the saint, and the historical figure are almost impossible to make. This is not to say the saint was entirely invented from myths of the goddess. It is

41 Baring-Gould believes the identification of Beon as Benignus to be a fantasy of William's annotators and the tombstone a blatant forgery (1907 vol.1: 204).

more likely that the girl Brigid was named after the goddess and then when the saint's fame grew, their stories became overlapped. Information from Saint Brigid's various *Lives* is certainly coloured by legends of the goddess; both were patrons of poetry, smithcraft and healing. She is honoured, conversely, as both a virgin and also as a mother, mixing elements of the goddess with the Virgin Mary. Despite being a virgin she also symbolises fertility. One story from the saint's *Life* tells of her dropping a vessel of water she had blessed without it breaking or spilling. Saint Patrick ordered the water to be divided amongst Ireland's main churches and the rest be sprinkled on the fields to promote fertile soil and a good harvest (Condren 1989: 73). Her association with the cycles of nature is also evident in her role as patroness of midwives.

Both the goddess and the saint are associated with fire and the sun; Saint Brigid is said to have hung her cloak on its rays. She is born at sunrise, neither within nor without a house, and imagery of her features flames above her head as they did the goddess (Condren 1989: 65-6). The Romano-British equivalent of the goddess would be Sulis-Minerva, who is honoured at Bath; and Brighid is also equated by some with fire goddess Brigantia. The convent at Kildare founded by Brigid housed a perpetual flame tended to by her nuns, much the same as those attended on the continent by the priestesses in the temples of the goddess Minerva (Condren 1989: 57).[42] The symbol of the saint, the 'Brigid's cross', a rush cross made traditionally on her feast day of 1st February, may have evolved from a pagan sun wheel symbol, although in the saint's story it is woven by Brigid to explain the Passion and was hung in houses to ward off evil. Her feast day occurs on the Celtic fire festival of Imbolc as well as the Roman Lupercalia, and later the Christian festival of Candlemas. These different traditions share similar rites for this day involving the lighting of candles, symbolically shining light into the darkness that came before. The 'Brighid's cross' may have been used in earlier times to usher in the

42 Similarities may also be drawn with the Graeco-Roman priestesses of Hestia/Vesta who lived communally and tended a perpetual flame. Perhaps the idea of the 'Vestal Virgins' may be what inspired the convent at Kildare to keep Brigid's flame. The virginity of the servants of Vesta was fiercely protected and symbolised the fruitfullness of the land, and this is echoed in the *Lives* of Brigid. (See story about the dropped water vessel) (Condren 1989: 68-73). Gerald of Wales tells us that the nuns at Kildare numbered nineteen plus Brigid herself and remained nineteen after she was gone. They worked around a twenty day cycle, upon the last day of which they left the tending of the fire to the absent Brigid herself, always finding it miraculously still lit the next day.

sun after winter.

The *Lives* of Brigid tell us she was born to an Irish lord, Dubtach, and to Brotseach, a slave in his house. His jealous wife ordered Brotseach's removal and she was sent away and sold to a druid in Meath, at whose home Brigid was born. She was treated kindly here, but not received so kindly on returning to her father's house when she was grown, being continually scolded and beaten by her wicked stepmother in true folkloric fashion. She returned to the house of the druid when her mother became ill, taking on her duties and eventually winning her mother's freedom from the druid and his wife. On returning to her father she narrowly escaped being sold to Dunlang, son of the king of Leinster. Whilst her father was inside negotiating terms, Brigid was left outside in his chariot. She was approached by a poor begging leper, and having nothing else to give him, gave away her father's valuable sword. On hearing this, Dunlang sent them away, refusing to take on someone who would give away possessions so freely. The angry Dubtach next tried to marry her off but Brigid refused and was eventually allowed to enter a convent. She was veiled by Bishop Macchille at Usny Hill in Meath, who clothed her in white and she thenceforth resided with seven other virgins, each representing a beatitude, Brigid choosing that of Mercy, a quality she was famed for during her life. She was also famous for brewing fine ale which was much sought after by the poor, so much so that on one occasion she had to tell them bluntly that the only ale she had to give them was her bath water. This is more likely an example of her dry humour than the miracle that it was made into, in which she turned bathwater into beer!

As well as being dry-witted, Brigid was known for her forceful nature and would recruit girls from a very young age to join Holy Orders. She was afraid of no one and would chastise those who refused hospitality or were wasteful. She scolded her father for beating his maids, after which, Dubtach asked Brigid for help in recovering his lost sword which had found its way into the hands of the son of Dunlang, Iollan, now King of Leinster. Brigid travelled to the King and asked for the sword in return for eternal life and the continuation of his royal lineage. Iollan, although baptised, only pretended to Christianity and scoffed at her offer.

Above: St. Brigid: This depiction of the Irish saint blends in the traditions of the goddess Brighid that were synonymous with Saint Brigid, including the flames above her head and the distinctive Brighid's Cross. Acrylic on canvas (15.5in x 20in).

Instead he asked for a long life, victory over his enemies and had Brigid join him in battle, cursing his enemies from her chariot, which she did without fear. Having earned the respect of this king she was granted a piece of land on which to build her monastery for both sexes, a haven for those who felt no call to arms in a time that was filled with war (Baring-Gould and Fisher 1907 vol.1: 268-76).

The monastery at Kildare that housed the sacred flame was possibly a previous pagan sacred site or even a school of Druidry, which was later turned over to Christian use.[43] She is said to have set the boundaries by spreading her cloak as far as it would reach (Condren 1989: 67). Some interpret this a miracle, others glean from it the wiliness of the saint, who may actually have unravelled the cloak and pegged out the thread to give herself a substantial plot of land! Kildare soon became established as one of the major seats of religion in Ireland and devotion to Brigid spread over the country. Amongst her friends and contemporaries were counted Gildas, who sent her a hand bell from his home in Brittany; Bishop Erc of Slane, with whom she travelled to Munster (the same Erc who came to Cornwall with Breaca et al.); and possibly St. Patrick in his late years, for whom she is said to have woven a funereal winding sheet (Baring-Gould and Fisher 1907 vol.1: 281).

Traditions survive in Wales and Brittany of visits from the popular saint. Several churches and towns in Devon and Somerset also bear her name.[44] So also we have the legend of her coming to Glastonbury. Baring-Gould postulates that the legend of Brigid being at Glastonbury may have been born from the memory of there being a house affiliated with Kildare there (1907 vol.1: 264). William of Malmesbury tells us that she arrived in 488 CE, shortly after Patrick's death and established a nunnery at Beckery where she stayed for a while before returning to Ireland, leaving behind a bag of treasures including her bell, necklace, and embroidering kit (Lewis 1925: 19-20). Brigid may

also have inspired the stone carvings on the tower of St.

43 The name Kildare is derived from *Cill Dara,* meaning 'church of the oak'. The great oak near which the monastery was built is mentioned in Brigid's *Life* and was a tree sacred to the druids, hinting at the possibility of an earlier druid school at this site.

44 Devon has Bridestowe and Bridgerule, and Somerset has churches at Breane and Chelvey. Seventeen churches are dedicated to her in Wales as either St. Bride or St. Ffraid. Baring-Gould believes the Brigid active in South Wales to be a distinct and separate saint, Brigid of Cill-Muine, who absorbed the fame of her namesake (1907 vol.1: 285-6).

Michael's church on the Tor, still surviving to this day, of a woman milking a cow. She is depicted in a 1920s window in St. John's Church on Glastonbury High Street accompanied by a tame wolf. This presumably is a reference to the story of Brigid befriending a wolf to replace the pet wolf of the king, which had been mistakenly killed by one of his subjects whose life was forfeit as a result until Brigid arrived to pacify the king with the replacement.

The oratory where she stayed, said to have been dedicated to St. Mary Magdalene, gave way to a larger chapel dedicated to Brigid herself after her departure. Archaeological digs at the site, known as 'Bride's Mound', uncovered the remains of these chapels and another building, possibly a priests house or postulated to even be Brigid's own dwelling.[45] The chapel at Beckery became entwined with the Arthurian myth when John of Glastonbury, writing circa 1400, identified it as a place King Arthur was told to visit in a dream. On entering the chapel he had a vision of the Virgin Mary holding the infant Jesus and she gave to him a crystal cross, which he gave to the Abbot of Glastonbury (and which subsequently became lost). From this day forth he abandoned the Pendragon banner and replaced it with one depicting the Madonna and Child.

Brigid returned to Ireland and is widely accepted to have died in Ulster around the year 525 aged seventy although other estimates range from age seventy-four to eighty-four. It is interesting that, unlike the legends of other foreign saints associated with the south-west, Glastonbury only claims to have housed the belongings of Brigid, not the body. This gives credence to the integrity of William's account. In his earlier 'Acts of the Kings of England' he states that he does not know the fate of Brigid, whether she died at Glastonbury or returned home. After researching his Glastonbury tome he concludes that she did return home and it is added by later

---

45 The excavation of the early timber monastery at Beckery in the 1960s shows the graves to contain all male bodies except for one female and two children, meaning it was likely a male monastic community. The second stone chapel shows a curious hole in the wall, perhaps to house a staircase to a gallery where the relics of Brigid were displayed or possibly the hole of legend through which pilgrims were passed to gain forgiveness for their sins. A later medieval chapel overlayed the Saxon one, dating to around the thirteenth century (Rahtz 1993: 151-6). The 'priest's house' accompanied this chapel, being therefore impossible to have belonged to Brigid of Kildare. However we cannot rule out the possibility of it belonging to one of the other St Brigids active in Britain at later times and their association with places being later attributed to Brigid of Kildare.

hands that she died in Ireland, suggesting that the monks were not entirely unscrupulous in their additions and alterations for they could easily have announced her to be buried at Beckery (Lewis 1925: 22).

William of Malmesbury also mentions, somewhat cautiously, the visits of St. Columba and St. Gildas to Glastonbury, and more confidently, of the patronage of St. **David**. The original author of St David's *Life* believed the Old Church at Glastonbury to have been built by David's hands, which would be anachronistic with other accounts. William instead suggests David travelled to re-dedicate the church but after receiving a vision from Jesus who told him the church had already been dedicated to His mother the Virgin Mary by His own hands, he set about building and dedicating a new church instead. He gifted Glastonbury with a sapphire-inlaid travelling altar that he obtained in Jerusalem. This was believed to have survived at the Abbey up until the dissolution when it was confiscated by Henry VIII. Although David was most certainly buried in West Wales, William speculated that his relics were later brought to Glastonbury and mingled with those of St. Patrick in the Old Church in 946 (Lewis 1925: 24-9), however they were reported as being still in Wales in 1173 when Henry II made a pilgrimage there (Baring-Gould and Fisher 1907 vol.2: 314).

William also tells of Saint **Indract,** an Irishman who visited Patrick's tomb at Glastonbury and who was murdered nearby. Our only other sources are the anonymous author of the *Passion of St Indract,* who claimed his work to have been based on an Old English source, and John of Glastonbury, who took up the story and was influenced by both William and the *Passion.* John tells how, following their pilgrimage to Patrick's tomb, Indract and his companions were ambushed by Saxons at Shapwick (the *Passion* gives Huish Episcopi). The wicked men believed the holy company's brass-tipped staves to be gold and their purses to be stuffed with coins, not herbs, and so killed them for their perceived riches. The tale is set in the late seventh to early eighth centuries, the time of King Ine, who was holding court nearby and was responsible for the translation of the bodies to Glastonbury once he had heard of the sacrilege committed by his subjects. Indract was said to have been buried on the left of the altar next to Patrick.

Above: The Saints of Glastonbury: This Celtic-inspired illustration shows some of Glastonbury's iconic locations – Chalice Well, Wearyall Hill, the Tor, and the Abbey, surrounded by some of its legendary saints (clockwise from top): St. Michael, St, Brigid, St. Collen, St. Dunstan, and St. Joseph of Arimathea. Acrylic on canvas (19.5in x 19.5in).

Now we come to the most 'definitively Glastonian' saint (although technically Saxon rather than Celtic) for whom the evidence is most reliable. Saint **Dunstan** was born four miles outside Glastonbury around the year 909 and was educated by monks of the Abbey, later becoming a monk and abbot himself. He not only excelled in the field of religion but was a master craftsman and founded the traditions of bell making and clock making at the Abbey. A drawing that survives today in the 'Glastonbury Classbook' of a monk kneeling at the feet of Christ is thought to be a self-portrait attributed to Dunstan himself (Lewis 1925: 54). As a young man his determination and intelligence were recognised and his talents saw him being sent to the court of King Æthelstan, but his learned ways and popularity with the King and his ladies drew the envy of his contemporaries who accused him of witchcraft and saw him flung from court. He entered the house of the Bishop of Winchester after this who persuaded him to take vows of celibacy and become a monk, a decision not lightly made by the young Dunstan. With this he returned to Glastonbury, building a small cell adjacent to the Old Church where he worked on his smithcraft. It is here that the famous story of his altercation with the Devil is set. John of Glastonbury records the tale, in which the Devil came into Dunstan's workshop to tempt him. The steadfast saint plucked a pair of red hot iron tongs from the fire and pinched the Devil's nose with them, eliciting terrible howls of anguish from the Devil, whom he held for several hours before releasing![46]

In the following years, King Æthelstan was succeeded by his brother Edmund who also summoned Dunstan to court, which he was holding at nearby Cheddar. Again, Dunstan was plotted against by courtiers and sent away, although not without doubts by the King. Soon followed an incident in which it is told King Edmund was out hunting stags in the Mendip forest when his quarry and hounds went over a cliff into Cheddar Gorge. Edmund, believing his

---

46 Various versions of the story of St. Dunstan and the Devil exist in folklore from the eleventh century right up to the 19th, including a rhyme about it in Charles Dickens' 'A Christmas Carol'. In some versions the Devil tempts Dunstan in the form of a woman, in some he merely tries to engage him in bawdy conversation. In the nineteenth century poem 'The Horse Shoe: The True Legend of St Dunstan and the Devil' by Edward G. Flight, Satan hears Dunstan's harp playing and chimes in with hideous harmonies. The storyteller rejects the common motif of Dunstan pinching the Devil's nose and instead tells how the saint grasped the Devil's cloven hoof and hammered a burning hot horseshoe to it. This is claimed to be the origin of why horseshoes are lucky; that they were hung above doorways of dwellings to act as a reminder to the Devil of this episode and to keep him out.

horse to be about to follow the same fate, in those split seconds repented on his treatment of Dunstan and vowed to make things right if he was spared. Miraculously his horse swerved and avoided the steep drop. Edmund immediately sought Dunstan and appointed him as Abbot of Glastonbury (Lewis 1925: 55). Thus began a period of great monastic reform. Dunstan introduced the Rule of St. Benedictine to the Abbey under which it remained until its dissolution, and also expanded and enlarged the Abbey buildings. He subsequently spent a great amount of his time at the royal court as a royal advisor where he held considerable influence in the years after Edmund's death. His puritanical nature saw him expelled from the court for a third time, after which he fled to a Benedictine monastery in Ghent. He was not abroad for long, and was received back into the fold by a new king, Edgar, who appointed him Archbishop of Canterbury. A time of peace ensued in which Dunstan, with the full support of the king, pushed forward his ecclesiastical reforms, eventually retiring from court to teach at Canterbury.

Dunstan died in 988 and was recognised as a saint almost immediately. He was formally canonised in 1029. Dunstan was buried at Canterbury but during the sack of London and Kent in 1012 by the Danes, it is claimed his relics were removed to Glastonbury. William of Malmesbury wrote that four monks who had survived the massacre and escaped to Glastonbury, returned to rescue the remains of their leader. They were said to have brought him back and kept the exact location of his new tomb a secret, held and passed on to only one monk at a time, lest the relics be potentially uncovered and taken back by Canterbury in the future. It was after the Great Fire of 1184 that the relics were uncovered by the monks as a whole and moved to a new spot for veneration, as recorded in notes after William's death (Lewis 1925: 58-61). This of course begs the question of the authenticity of their claim, at a time when so many saints were being uncovered at or linked to Glastonbury, and a time when revenue for the Abbey was desperately needed. Neither his tomb at Glastonbury or at Canterbury survives so we can not say definitively, but it is only natural that the monks would wish to revere the great saint, who came from their own Abbey, within its walls. The collecting of relics by the Abbey did not however begin after the fire, it was an integral part of medieval monastic life at all holy sites and necessary to initiate a saint's cult that would draw in pilgrims (Rahtz 1993: 64-5). Glastonbury was far from unusual in this sense so its claims may have been seen as no more incredulous than any other monastery. Other saints whose relics were said to have been removed to Glastonbury for safe keeping from raiders include St. Illtyd, St. Aidan, St Hilda of Whitby, St. Benedict Bishop, St. Ceofrid, and the Venerable Bede, who were all brought by a Northumbrian abbot taking refuge during Dunstan's rule (Lewis 1925: 50).

What makes Glastonbury stand out from other monastic sites is its claim of most ancient foundation by **Joseph of Arimathea** in the first century CE, upon whose shoulders stand the other saints who have come to be associated with the area down the ages. The Gospels speak of Joseph as a rich man and secret disciple of Jesus who begged Pontius Pilate for Christ's body after the Crucifixion and who clothed and buried the body in the tomb which had been intended for himself. Later apocryphal texts such as the *Gospel of Nicodemus* further his story, telling of his imprisonment by Jewish elders for burying Jesus' body. This was expanded upon by medieval Grail romance author Robert de Boron who wrote that it was the Grail that sustained Joseph while he was in captivity. He, as its first keeper, sent it to Britain with his followers, an idea that was transformed by other writers into the Grail being brought by Joseph himself to England's shores.

The medieval claim of an apostolic foundation of the church in Britain before the one in Rome was likely inspired by early fourth century mentions by the likes of Eusebius that apostles of Jesus made it as far as Britain. The first mention of Joseph by name as the one to reach Britain is in the *Life of Mary Magdalene* from the ninth century. Details of the route Joseph and the other apostles took describe a trade route which may have given rise to the idea that Joseph was a merchant who had previously travelled to Britain. This theory, in its most developed form, has Joseph as the great-uncle of Jesus, bringing the young messiah on one of his trading trips, which inspired the famous poem-hymn by William Blake, speculating “and did those feet in ancient time, walk upon England's mountains green”?[47] Baring-Gould recorded in his 'Book

47 The theory of Jesus' coming to the South-west of Britain and possibly Glastonbury is linked to an idea from the Book of Revelation wherein it says Jesus will create a 'new Jerusalem', which serves as evidence for Glastonbury's claim as spiritual capital of Britain. Detractors may quote Bishop Irenaeus' second century list of Christian churches and its lack of mention of Britain as proof that no church existed there before Augustine. However, as John Michell points out, Irenaeus with his extreme views on heresies would likely have regarded any Celtic churches as semi-pagan deviations and not included them (1990: 77).

of Cornwall' a folkloric belief that "Joseph was in the tin trade" and that is what originally brought him to the South-West (1899: 57).[48] Assertion of Joseph's coming and his founding of the first church in Britain did not stay confined to annotations in the works of William of Malmesbury by the monks of Glastonbury but became widespread and popularly accepted, even being quoted by Queen Elizabeth I in her speech to Catholic bishops, asserting that Joseph brought Christianity to Britain long before Augustine did.

Joseph's association with Glastonbury is inextricably linked to King Arthur and the Grail legend. Later writers elaborating on Robert de Boron's Grail saga variously told of Joseph bringing the cup Christ used at the Last Supper or two cruets, one containing the blood and one the sweat of Christ, collected as he hung on the cross.[49] This legend became the focus for the Chalice Well (sometimes called the Blood Spring or Red Spring, close to another called the White Spring) where Joseph was rumoured to have buried his holy treasure. Pilgrims still flock to the spring daily to partake of the waters for its renowned holy healing properties. The symbol of the Vesica Piscis, two circles overlapping each other, has become associated with the Chalice Well, and has been described by some as representing the union of Heaven and Earth or Hieros Gamos - 'Sacred Marriage'[50].

---

48 The folkloric belief in Joseph as a tin trader may have been influenced by a misconception that Marazion in Cornwall is connected with refugees from Zion ie. Jerusalem and in a mistranslation of its earliest recorded name *Maragasiou* as 'Market Jew' (Berresford Ellis 1974: 140). It is however unusual that legends surrounding Marazion and the neighbouring St. Michael's Mount revolve largely around the Archangel and do not say much about Joseph or Jesus, who were more commonly said to have landed at Looe, Falmouth, or St.Just in Roseland.

49 The legend of the Holy Cruets comes from an obscure fragment attributed, John of Glastonbury tells us, to Melkinus, 'an Avalonian' whom he dates to 560 CE. The now lost text is regarded by most scholars as dubious in origin. Twentieth century writers Rev. Lionel Lewis and A. H. Lewis put stock in this text drawing from it the conclusion that not only is Joseph of Arimathea buried in the Old Church but his grave is above that of the Virgin Mary, who, having been brought to Britain herself by Joseph, lived and died at Glastonbury. These views however are generally seen as far fetched by even the most forgiving scholars.

50 The Vesica Piscis is a geometric symbol seen as sacred in several different traditions, from ancient Egypt to Kabbalah, Freemasonry and Astrology. The central shape created by the intersection of the circles has been interpreted as a form of yonic symbolism and named a *mandorla* in Italian, 'almond', for its shape. Religious paintings frequently feature this mandorla shape as a kind of aura around holy figures, notably Christ. The word *Vesica Piscis* literally means 'bladder of the fish' which is interesting considering the

Another relic still venerated at Glastonbury today is the Holy Thorn, believed to have sprung into bloom from Joseph's staff. Eighteenth-century records of local traditions tell that Joseph and his eleven companions landed south of the current town, coming by water, as much of the surrounding country was submerged at this time. They stopped to rest at Wirral or Wearyall Hill, as it is still known, Joseph proclaiming that they were "weary all" and thrusting his staff into the ground, where it promptly took root (Lewis 1924: 29).[51] By the mid-fourteenth century when John of Glastonbury was writing, Joseph and the Grail's connection to Glastonbury were firmly ensconced and accepted as part of its history. The abbots went as far as to adopt a coat of arms showing the two cruets beside a cross made of thorn twigs and interspersed with droplets representing the blood and sweat of Christ (Michell 1990: 94).

Christian symbol of the Ichthys fish can be found within its shape.

51 Other 'Holy Thorns' exist in Glastonbury, said to be descendants of the first, including one in the Abbey grounds and one in the churchyard of St. John's. The custom of sending a branch from the tree at Christmas time (when it would be in flower) to the monarch survived the Reformation and continued to the reign of Charles I when the original tree unfortunately fell at the hands of a Puritan. The custom was recently revived in modern times also (Lewis 1924: 33).

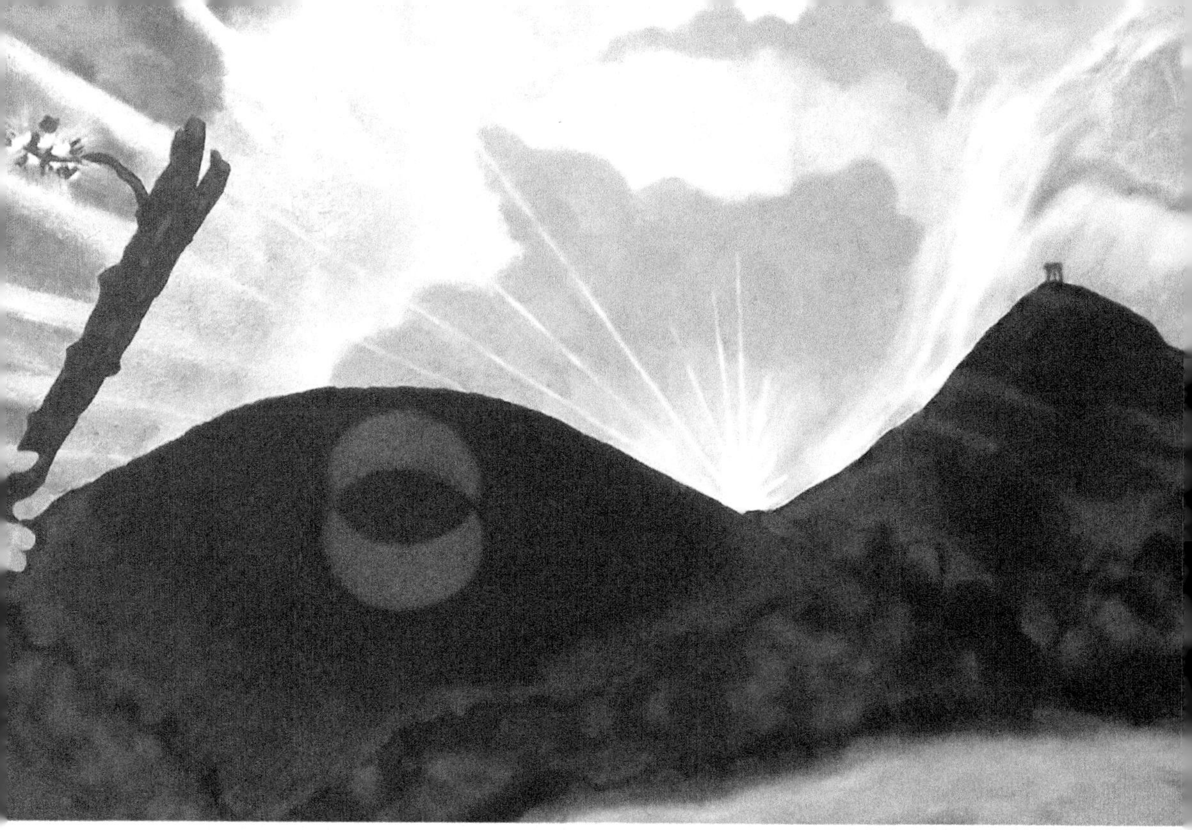

Above: Joseph of Arimathea: From the Holy Land, Joseph of Arimathea brings the fabled Grail to Avalon and plants his staff on Wearyall Hill where it takes root and begins to bloom. Acrylic on canvas (39in x 12in).

A lot of Grail legends sprang up around the 1180s, correspondent with the time of Glastonbury's Great Fire and the monks' subsequent discovery of the supposed graves of King Arthur and Guinevere in the grounds of the Abbey. The Grail romances incorporated both apocryphal material and characters and motifs from Celtic legend. In Chretien de Troyes' *Perceval,* the father of the Fisher King is a maimed king, wounded in the leg or groin by a lance, similar to the wound Christ received on the cross. The spear of Longinus and the spear that pierces the Wounded King become synonymous in later versions such as Wagner's *Parsifal.* The Fisher King becomes the brother-in-law of Joseph in Robert de Boron's *Joseph d'Arimathie* and is named Bron, reminiscent of the Celtic king Bran the Blessed from early Welsh texts, owner of a magical pre-Christian Grail-like vessel (Michell 1990: 92-3). In the story, at the house of the wounded king, Perceval sees a procession of a maiden bearing a grail, a soldier carrying a bleeding lance, and two boys carrying a candelabrum. Perceval fails to ask the critical question, who the grail serves, and therefore fails to heal the wounded king. The Perceval tale is replete with Celtic imagery: the head in the bowl of the Welsh version, *Peredur*, being reminiscent of the head of Bran which continued speaking after his beheading, the spear reminiscent of the Irish spear of Lugh, one of the 'Four Treasures of the Tuatha Dé Danann', and the curative powers of the Grail itself resembling Bran's magical cauldron or Horn of Plenty. Grail legends later became more Christianised, emphasising the Christian purity of the knights Galahad and Perceval and the flaws of secular chivalry represented by Lancelot. Medieval interest in genealogies and legitimacy is evident in the Grail knights claiming descent from Joseph of Arimathea.

After the Abbey fire, the monks perhaps recognised the growing popularity of the Arthurian legend and the pilgrims it could draw in. There was no previous mention of a link between Arthur and Glastonbury in the early works of William of Malmesbury, only the later rewrites. The first written connection is by Gerald of Wales who passed through Glastonbury shortly after the excavation and reports seeing the lead cross found with the bodies proclaiming them to be "the renowned King Arthur with Guinevere his second wife". Satisfied with the claim, he wrote in his *Liber de Principis Instructione* in the early 1190s that "What is now known as Glastonbury used, in ancient times to be called the Isle of Avalon". We may theorise nationalistic reasons behind his publicizing of the discovery of Arthur's body. Being of mixed Welsh and Norman descent and a great supporter of the Norman monarchy he was in the perfect position to publish proof of Arthur's actual death to the benefit of the Normans who wished to suppress potential Welsh uprisings inspired by the tradition that their ancient king was merely sleeping and would one day return to lead them. It has been suggested that with this in mind, the monks invited Gerald there as a witness to be fooled by their forgery and spread the word, therefore securing future revenue for the Abbey (Rahtz 1993: 56).

The fifteenth century *Morte d'Arthur* became the most central piece of Arthurian literature but whilst making use of the Glastonbury-as-Avalon claim, the author Sir Thomas Malory did not confirm or deny it. He has Arthur remove himself following the final battle to "the vale of Avilion to heal me of my grievous wound" to please the supporters of the sleeping king theory and then writes a scene in which Sir Bedivere comes across a hermit in a chapel in Glastonbury who used to be Archbishop of Canterbury (perhaps based upon Dunstan?) but had fled from Mordred's wrath. The hermit is interring a corpse that was brought to him by a number of ladies which Bedivere interprets as being Arthur but the truth of which Malory asserts the hermit does not know, leaving enough mystery to continue the Arthurian tradition at Glastonbury (1998: 516-7).

The prominent feature of the Glastonbury landscape that is the Tor inextricably links the Celtic, the Arthurian and the saints' traditions.[52] Not only is this grand hill a station of St **Michael** the Archangel, as mentioned in the previous chapter, it is also a symbolic entrance to the Underworld or Otherworld and one of the places the sleeping Arthur is said to be located. In several Arthurian romances, based on a tale in the *Life of Gildas,* Guinevere is abducted by Melwas, a Somerset king who takes her to his fortress on the Tor in the *Isle of Glass.* John Michell equates this with a Celtic version of the Greek abduction of Persephone to the Underworld by Hades (1990: 24). Another early Arthurian abduction story, in *Culhwch and Olwen,* tells of the lord of Annwn (the Otherworld), Gwyn ap Nudd, and his abduction of his sister, a matter settled by Arthur. Arthur travels to the Otherworld, which is therein described as a glass fortress in *The Spoils of Annwn,* seeking a proto-Grail, a magic cauldron. In later stories Gwyn is a psychopomp and leader of the mythical Wild Hunt, and the entrance to his Otherworld becomes definitively fixed at Glastonbury in the sixteenth century *Life of St.Collen.*

After several adventures, including engaging in single combat with a pagan and receiving a relic from the Pope, **Collen** retired to Glastonbury, where he took Holy Orders and rose to the rank of abbot.[53] He travelled around spreading the Christian word for several years but grew angry at the irreligious ways of men and secluded himself in a cell near the base of Glastonbury Tor. One day, the rather hot-headed saint heard two men outside discussing Gwyn ap Nudd who was king of the Fairies and, disapproving of their topic, came out to chastise them and tell them that these were demons they spoke of. The men told him he would have to answer to Gwyn and sure enough he soon received an invite to speak with Gwyn atop the Tor. Collen refused the messenger three times but

52 Arthurian legend was intimately linked with saints' *Lives* from an early age. Arthur is mentioned in seven saints' *Lives* thought to have been written pre-Geoffrey of Monmouth, the first author to popularize the cult of Arthur (Tatlock 1939: 345-65). These include Cadoc, Carantoc, and Padarn. Arthur is often shown as a tyrant in these stories and at odds with the saints, belying his early origins as a war leader rather than a gracious king.

53 It is mentioned that on returning from the continent Collen landed at and passed through Cornwall. This is probably in reference to the church of Saint Colan in Cornwall as an explanation for the place name.

was warned it would be worse for him if he did not go, so armed with a vial of holy water he proceeded to climb the hill. On reaching the top he discovered a grand castle, attended by the most beautiful men and women and filled with delightful food and harmonious music. Inside he was courteously greeted by the king who offered Collen whatever food or comforts his heart desired. Collen staunchly refused and sprinkled the table with his holy water, and upon doing so, the banquet, the people, and the entire castle vanished.

Baring-Gould likens Collen's role in this curious story to that of Michael the Archangel, patron of the Tor's church, suppressing the pagan forces surrounding the Tor (Baring-Gould and Fisher 1907 vol.2: 158-60). The *Life* is indeed replete with pagan imagery, reminiscent of some of the much earlier saints' *Lives*. Interestingly, it is only this sixteenth-century Welsh source that links Collen with Glastonbury; Collen is not among the many saints claimed to have been there by William of Malmesbury. It is curious that, in the *Life*, explanations are given of the saint's other dedications at Colan, in Cornwall and Llangollen in North Wales, yet such a colourful and memorable episode occurs in Somerset where Collen has no dedications. Perhaps by this time the gravitas of the 'Glastonbury connection' was a draw for writers from further afield and the trend for linking prominent saints to the place such as David and Columba proved too tempting for Collen's Welsh biographers, despite the doubtful historical basis.

Right: St. Michael: Icon showing St. Michael in his aspect of dragon slayer, subduing the forces of the Underworld. Acrylic and gold leaf on wood (14.5in x 11in).

As we have seen, the end of the twelfth century proved to be a real turning point for Glastonbury, when its fame really began to grow and shape its mythic landscape. Too much may be made of trying to separate history from legend and discover 'true facts' about Glastonbury's past. It would seem that there are many truths, many discourses woven together that seem to work in harmony with each other in this unique town and the scholar that tries to pull apart the threads to separate the pieces may well end up with nothing but tatters. A lot of effort is put into proving that parts of the Abbey's heritage were forged but does this destroy the spiritual devotion that was afforded to these figures? No. This is the part that is most definitely 'real' and undeniable. The wise know not to take the details from a saint's *Life* to be a true historical account, any more than they would a parable. The multi-layered, multi-faceted spiritual habitat of Glastonbury has without doubt been a comfort to seekers throughout the ages and will undoubtedly continue to do so...

Chapter 5

A Dumnonian Family of Saints

If we think about the map of Cornwall as being dominated in the north by Welsh saintly migrants as far south as Liskeard, and Irish saints in the south-west as far east as Perranporth, it is easy to miss some of the pockets in-between where we find some wholly Cornish saints. As we have seen, it appears to be a popular fashion for the authors of saints' *Lives* to give the subject of their writing an Irish or Welsh origin to add credence or authenticity to their 'saintliness', perhaps because of the respected existing monastic schools in these regions. There is, however, an important family of saints within Cornwall whose influence was not only spiritual but regal. They are also tied by marriage into the family of Welsh Patron Saint David and through literature into the Arthurian legend.

We begin by examining Constantine, or more precisely **Constantine Gorneu** - 'The Cornish'. As Constantine was a popular name amongst rulers of the time, it is often that scholars confuse the disparate figures. This is not the tyrant Constantine who was berated by Gildas[54], converted by Saint Petroc, and who became the namesake of Constantine Bay but rather his great- great-grandfather. This earlier Constantine is believed by some to be the man traditionally labelled Tyrannus and usurper; a soldier who was elevated through the ranks to become Western Roman Emperor Constantine III[55]. He ruled from 407 to 411, when he and his son

---

54 Gildas, a contemporary and relation of the later Constantine berated the king in his *De Excidio et Conquestu Britanniae* amongst four other rulers whom he unfavourably compared to Biblical beasts.

55 It is alleged Constantine was only chosen by the legions in Britain to be Western Roman Emperor due to his name, or rather his namesake,

Constans, whom he had raised to the level of co-emperor, were executed. Others prefer to associate him with Cystennin Fendigaid "the Blessed", the Welsh son of Macsen Wledig (Roman Emperor Magnus Maximus) and St. Helen ferch Eudaf (Elen Luyddog "of the Hosts")[56]. The *Genealogies*, however, suggest him to be the son of Conomor, King of Dumnonia.

The difficulty for modern scholars stems from the influence of the popular pseudo-history of Geoffrey of Monmouth, *Historia Regum Britanniae* on other writers, in which he creates a fictional king by combining Constantine the Usurper with Arthurian legend. Geoffrey allocates not only Constans as his son but also Ambrosius Aurelianus and Uther Pendragon. Thus follows a highly fictional account, weaving in the already infamous character of Vortigern, who ingratiated himself with Constans, and after Constantine's death (murdered by a Pictish vassal) took over governance of the country, as Constans had been cloistered in a monastery for most of his life and had no knowledge of how to rule. After weaselling his way into power, Vortigern invited a great number of Picts into King Constans' court knowing full well of their treacherous behaviour, and allowed them to kill the young king, taking the crown for himself. Young Ambrosius and Uther Pendragon fled to Brittany, only to return years later with an army to regain their rightful throne. Although also a tale of treachery and supplantation, this does not bear much relation to the historic events recorded about the Emperor and his son Constans. Ambrosius and Constantine the Usurper were most definitely historical figures but their parentage is uncertain beyond being Romano-British and as such they appear to have been 'sandwiched in' to the family tree of Constantine Gorneu. This inaccurate family tree took root in later medieval literature, despite not matching historical accounts, and influenced many authors right down to the modern day.

Welsh genealogies the *Bonedd y Saint* and the *Jesus College MS 20* credit Constantine Gorneu with two saintly sons **Erbin** and Digain, who both have dedications in Denbighshire; Erbin at Erbistock, near Wrexham, and Digain at Llangernyw, the village name pointing to Digain's Cornish origins – 'church site of the Cornishman'. Close to here is Llangystennin, although whether this dedication belongs to Constantine the Cornish, the Blessed, or

---

Constantine the Great, first Christian Emperor. as a kind of 'good luck charm'.
56 Who in turn is often mistaken for Constantine the Great, son of another Helen, Elen ferch Coel.

Constantine the Great is still debated. We are concerned with Erbin, who, besides his Welsh dedication, may be the patron of two Cornish sites, both in mid Cornwall, St. Erme north of Truro and St. Ervan situated between Newquay and Padstow. Although both churches were dedicated to the second century Greek martyr Saint Hermes from the thirteenth century, doubt is cast by the fact that William of Worcester records a 'Saint Hermes, confessor of the people of Cornwall' suggesting that despite the latinization, the local people regarded this Hermes as a Cornish saint, and therefore possibly stems from the king called Erbin.

Next we come to his son, **Geraint ab Erbin**[57], also known as Gerrans, and latinised as Gerontius. A peculiarity of Geraint's family tree occurs if we take Geraint's grandfather Constantine Gorneu to be one and the same with the Emperor Constantine III. The Roman leader had a general named Gerontius in command of his army. Gerontius was sent to Spain along with the newly appointed co-emperor, Constans, son of Constantine. It was here Gerontius revolted and slew Constans, proclaiming Maximus as Emperor instead. If Erbin was actually a younger sibling of Constans it would seem unusual for him to give his son the same name as the man who betrayed his father and murdered his brother!

Geraint is remembered more as a Dumnonian king and warrior than as a saint. He was mentioned in early Welsh literature in the poem *Geraint, Son of Erbin* which features in the thirteenth century *Black Book of Carmarthen* but may be as old as tenth century in its composition. The poem is significant in being the earliest mention of Arthur as Emperor. It is also the first to position Arthur in Cornwall[58]. It tells of Geraint's deeds at the Battle of Llongborth, variously said to be Portsmouth, Langport in Somerset, or Penbryn beach in Cardigan. His subsequent death is believed to be circa 475 but ranges up to 510 in other accounts. Geraint ab Erbin is

---

57 Other recorded sons of Erbin include Ysgin, in the *Bonedd y Saint,* and Dyfel and Ermid in *Culhwch and Olwen* (variously also spelt Dywel and Erinid) are listed alongside Geraint. David Nash Ford believes Dywel may be identical with Domuel, the given name for the father of St. Piran (see Chapter 3).

58 August Hunt speculates that the formulaic repetition of Geraint's name and exclusion of any other names besides the one mention of Arthur's could be taken to mean Geraint embodied the legendary king rather than was accompanied by him (Hunt, 2010: 98-100). The Anglo-Saxon Chronicle records a battle which could be Llongborth, between the Saxons against a Geraint of Cornwall, as occurring in 710, but this is far too late for it to have involved our Geraint, or indeed Arthur, so may be a different battle and different Geraint.

mentioned as *Geraint Llyngesoc,* one of the three head of fleets that patrolled the West coast against Saxon invaders (Baring-Gould and Fisher 1907 vol.3: 47-8).

He is more famously featured in the prose romance *Geraint and Enid,* one of five Arthurian tales and 'Three Welsh Romances' which comprise part of the *Mabinogion.* Although recorded in Middle-Welsh they are likely to have stemmed from the continental romances of Chrétien de Troyes or at least shared a common source. Many scholars believe due to its similarities to Chrétien's *Erec et Enid,* the story was transplanted and the hero merely given a name Welsh audiences would recognise.

The romance begins with Geraint setting out to avenge a slight to one of Queen Gwenhwyfar's maidens. He tracked down the discourteous knight Edeyrn ab Nudd to the town of Cardiff where he was attending a tourney at a grand castle. Geraint was welcomed into the run-down home of the castle's former lord, who had been dispossessed of his fortune by his nephew. Geraint borrowed an old and rusty lance and armour from the old man and took on the arrogant knight in the tourney for the title 'Knight of the Sparrow-Hawk' and to win the hand of the old man's daughter, Enid. Geraint was victorious over the knight and obtained his promise that he would go and make amends for his insult to the Queen. He also succeeded in persuading the young earl to return his uncle's possessions and in winning Enid's hand in marriage.

Geraint was soon recalled from Arthur's court at Caerleon by his father Erbin (who is mentioned as Arthur's uncle) to help defend Cornwall's borders. Although reluctant, Geraint complied, and before long gained fame as a successful and skilful knight. Wealth and riches came to the Cornish palace and life became easy for Geraint. So easy, in fact, that his courtiers began to joke behind his back about how their king preferred to spend his days indoors with his wife. On hearing these rumours, Enid was saddened, and lamented causing her husband's softness, weeping over his sleeping body. Geraint, awoken by this, misunderstood her words, taking from them that she wished for some 'other' brave and warlike knight. He rose and vowed to prove his worth to his wife, and had their horses saddled.

Geraint took Enid out on a dangerous path through the forest but bade her ride in front and not to speak one word to him, therefore rendering her unable to explain his mistake. Their route took them into the path of many bandits who would have taken both Geraint's wife and his horse and armour from him. Each time,

Enid tried to warn her husband of what lay ahead but he would not hear her words; still each time Geraint's fighting prowess prevailed and he killed their attackers. This happened several times, as they travelled through dangerous lands and Geraint continued to seek out the challenge of various knights, despite being wounded and weary. Even King Arthur was unable to divert Geraint from his mission. Finally, after a near fatal encounter with a giant, Geraint was taken to the house of a local earl who tried to console Enid with food and drink but she refused a single morsel until her husband, who lay close to death, was able to eat with her. The earl grew impatient with Enid and hit her on the ear, causing her to scream. The sound revived Geraint who found his sword and rushed over, avenging his wife with a brutal blow to the lord's head. In this moment Geraint realised his wife had been true to him all along and he was sorry for making her suffer through their journey. No part of the story refers to Geraint's status as a saint or any religious calling and is a purely secular tale extolling the benefits and drawbacks of knightly pride.

Another Geraint is mentioned in the *Life of St Teilo.* Teilo was passing through Cornwall and was received and sheltered by a king Gerrenius, to whom he promised he would return to give communion on his deathbed. This he did, bringing with him a stone sarcophagus which was dragged ashore at Dingereint, the circular fort in the parish of Gerrans, in the picturesque Cornish peninsula of Roseland. The Geraint in the *Life* is possibly a grandson of Geraint ab Erbin, who fought in the Battle of Catraeth and is mentioned in *Y Gododdin* as Geraint Rac Dehau – 'for the South'. The parish church in Gerrans is most likely dedicated to this later Geraint[59]. There was a cult of St. Géran in Brittany but without any information of his origin we are again unsure which Geraint this stems from.

The *Iolo Manuscripts* give us five sons of Geraint ab Erbin – Cador, Iestyn, Cyngar, Selyf and Caw[60]. The *Bonedd y Saint* states

---

59 The later king Gerrenius was supposedly buried with a horde at Carne Beacon in Veryan but no such treasure has ever been found. Other places in Roseland recall his name including Polgerran Wood.

60 The *Iolo Manuscripts* are a posthumous collection of works by eighteenth/nineteenth century Welsh Antiquarian Iolo Morganwg. The genealogies in the *Iolo Manuscripts*, whilst being regarded as genuine at the time, have been critiqued as being a mass of bit-translations and fantasies of Iolo's own making, but were still used for reference for important works such as Lady Charlotte Guest's translation of the *Mabinogion*, albeit not relied on for factual evidence.

that these are the children of his wife, Gwyar ferch Amlawdd, not his sweetheart Enid. Some manuscripts name a daughter, Silwen, but this is probably a mistake for Selyf. Other legends mention Breaca as a sister of Saint Levan but there is more evidence for her origin being Irish rather than Cornish. This generation of the family is where we begin to see more definitive saints, with their own *Lives* or mentions in the *Lives* of others.

Saint **Just** has two foundations in Cornwall. St. Just-in-Roseland from the eleventh century and St. Just-in-Penwith from 1291. Some historians believe these sites to be dedicated to two different saints. The two foundations are undeniably very different in character. The church of St. Just-in-Roseland is tucked away in a picturesque little valley near the entrance to the River Fal and is almost invisible until stumbled upon. Folk legend tells that this is the place Jesus first set foot in Britain when visiting with Joseph of Arimathea.

The church in St. Just-in-Penwith although less grand is undeniably ancient in its foundation, with religious buildings on its site from as early as the fifth century, or so is claimed by the church's literature. This view is aided by its curving western boundary wall which may follow the line of an early bank and ditch system. Unlike Roseland, its position is exposed and windy and could be described as 'handsome' rather than beautiful or picturesque. Although lacking the grand legend associated with Roseland, Penwith is claimed to have housed the relics of Saint Just as recorded by William of Worcester in 1478 where he is named 'St. Justus Martyr'[61].

Although one might expect early holy men such as Just to have been meek and mild, their legends suggest otherwise. Robert Hunt wrote in the nineteenth century about a large mass of granite that stands out in Penwith. The local legend was that Just had a neighbour to the south named Senan with whom he would repeatedly quarrel, and that this boulder was the result of a physical fight where Senan and Just launched huge rocks at each other! Two of the rocks they threw were said to have met in an almighty crash and fused together (Hunt 1903: 205). One might expect to find this kind of behaviour in a tale of two giants rather than two saints, and perhaps that is where the origins of the story

61 Drew takes this to mean he was amongst the company martyred by King Teudar, and supports the theory of Just's Irish origin (Drew 1824 vol2: 352-3). See footnote 11.

may be found.

Another saint with whom Just had an altercation was Keverne, who lived down on the Lizard peninsula. The story goes that Just went to visit Keverne and after he had left to return home, Keverne found one of his belongings missing, a bowl or plate or other such item. Keverne hurried along Just's trail, taking three large stones with him as ammunition, and caught up with him in the vicinity of Breage and Germoe. He allegedly hurled the stones at Just, making him drop the stolen goods, and chased him off. The stones are still by the roadside to this day[62].

Close by in Penwith is the well of Venton East, East being a variation of Iestyn/Just/Ust. The recorded Middle Cornish name for St. Just-in-Penwith in 1396 was Lanust, and in Wales we find a St. Ust, patron of Llanwrin, and also supposedly of a ruined church of Llanyst near Fishguard[63]. In Gwynedd and Anglesey we find two Llaniestyns, the latter of which houses a highly prized fourteenth-century stone effigy of Iestyn. These, too, are thought to be dedicated to the same son of Geraint, and probably secondary to his primary cult centre in Cornwall. Both sites also had holy wells associated with them; the Gwynedd well was famed for curing female illnesses and the Anglesey well earned a reputation as a cursing well, from a custom of throwing in pennies used to cover the eyes of the deceased (Breverton 2000: 331), although how these traits relate to the saint, if at all, we do not know.

The church in St. Just-in-Penwith houses an inscribed memorial stone, discovered during nineteenth-century restorations built into the wall and believed due to its epigraphy to date to the fifth or sixth century. It bears a Chi-Ro monogram, and the inscription 'SELVS IC IACET' translated as 'Selus lies here'. Two additional letters 'NI' appear above the name, and have been suggested to be either a correction on the part of the stonemason or possibly added by another later hand as an early form of graffiti to read Selus Ni Ic Iacet' (Selus does not lie here). This stone is widely believed to commemorate Saint Just's brother Selyf, also

62 As recorded by Richard Polwhele in the nineteenth century (1816: 59).
63 There is in eastern Cornwall also a village of Laneast, although Nicholas Orme believes this to be unrelated to the Iestyn of western Cornwall, particularly because the earliest dedication we have of the church there is to Saint Sidwell (Orme 2000: 155).

Above: St. Just-in-Roseland: Here St. Just stands outside his modern-day church in the Roseland peninsula, a representation of the sacred significance attached to place, which is still tangible at these saints' settlements today. Acrylic on canvas (15.5in x 12in).

known as Salomon, Selevan, and Levan who is to be found at the nearby village of St. Levan[64]

---

64 Rev. Baring-Gould theorises that Saint Levan and Just of Penwith were not the Selyf and Just of our Dumnonian family tree but gives them Irish origins - Just, son of Fergus, who was made Deacon Justinus of Fidarta, and Loebhan, metal worker of St Patrick. His reasoning for this is the abundance of Irish saintly foundations in the West Penwith region and its distance from the other Roseland cult centre. Also he gives Justinus as the preceptor of Ciaran of Saighir, i.e. Piran, another Irish migrant to Cornwall, so if we take his hypothesis to its logical conclusion Justinus also arrived with the saintly band of Irish. Other authors are less certain and usually accept the sites to be founded by the sons of Geraint. Orme names the patron of St. Levan as Silvanus in the fourteenth century, a latinised form of Selevan, itself a vernacular form of Salamon (Orme 1996: 97). Baring-Gould prefers Lansallos as a site of Salamon due to its proximity to Duloe, whose patron was his son

Most of the legends involving Saint **Levan** revolve around fishing. His chapel and holy well, not far along the coast from the modern open-air Minack Theatre, were supposed to be where he sat and fished. In a story gathered for Robert Hunt's tales of Cornwall, Saint Levan passed by the garden of a local woman called Johannah who criticised Levan for fishing for his supper on a Sunday to which the allegedly grumpy saint replied it was no different from her gathering her meal from her garden and for this he cursed the woman and any born in the parish with her name thereafter to be doomed to stupidity, henceforth it is alleged no Joannas have been registered in the parish for fear of Levan's curse. However maybe the woman was right in her criticism, as something later happened which may have been as a result of his refusing to fast on the Sabbath. He was one evening sat on his usual rock where he fished, when he felt a tug on his line and reeling it in, found two chad on the one hook. Requiring only one for himself and being unable to choose, he threw both back into the sea. Reeling his line in a second time he found the same two fish had returned to his hook. He cast them back again but a third time they caught on his line. Taking this as a sign, he returned home with both fish, where he discovered his sister had come to pay him a visit with two children, who had walked miles and were famished[65]. Saint Levan happily cooked the extra fish for them and blessed its appearance to provide for his guests.

However, tragedy struck and in their haste the hungry children failed to remove the bones and both choked to death. A bench end in the church shows two fish, perhaps commemorating this story. Another peculiarity of the church is the stone which stands in the churchyard named the 'St. Levan Stone' and may be a relic of pre-Christian worship at the site. The associated legend says St. Levan struck the large boulder, splitting it in two and uttering the prophecy "When with panniers astride, a pack-horse one can ride, through St. Levan's Stone, the world will be done" (Hunt 1903: 266). Hunt reported no discernible movement over 50 years and to this day the gap between the rock is only wide enough for the average

---

Cuby, and also Morval, belonging to his wife Wenna, and Pelynt, belonging to his sister-in-law Non. However this 'church of Salwys' has only ever been recorded as dedicated to Ildiern/a, possibly a bishop Hyldren. Curiously, Porthleven in Cornwall is not identified with Levan but with Elwyn.

65 Hunt records that Levan's sister was Breaca, although no correlation exists in other records linking these two Irish and Cornish saints.

person to walk through so may be some way off accommodating a laden pack horse! Selevan was said to have married St. Wenna (Gwen)[66] and fathered amongst others Saint Cuby (Cybi in Welsh). Whereas the Welsh genealogies are firm on the accepted lineage running back Cybi ap Salamon ap Geraint ap Erbin ap Custennin Gorneu, the thirteenth century Life of Cybi gives an alternate pedigree, switching the positions of Erbin and Geraint and replacing Custennin with Lud[67]. Being later in origin than the Welsh genealogies, and in direct disagreement with famous older texts such as *Geraint, Son of Erbin*, we can only assume this is a mistake. Salamon is also described differently in the *Life of Cuby*. It mentions Salamon to be a military leader, ie. King. Some believe Salamon to have succeeded his cousin Mark to the throne, which contrasts our image of the simple fisherman of St. Levan, and perhaps is why some regard Salamon and Levan as separate saints.

---

66 It should be noted that this Wenna is not the daughter of Brychan mentioned in Chapter 1 but Wenna daughter of Cynyr Ceinfarfog of Caer Goch, an Irish lord who colonised Dyfed.

67 The author may have gathered this name from King Lac, the father of Geraint's counterpart in *Erec et Enid* or from Geoffrey of Monmouth's King Lud, the legendary founder of London (Baring-Gould and Fisher, 1907 vol2: 203).

Above: St. Levan: St.Levan, shown as a humble fisherman on the beach of Porthchapel, close to his holy well and church. The wooden panels represent the story of St. Levan and the two fish. Acrylic on canvas (12in x 35 in).

Cuby's *Life* tells us he left Cornwall at the age of 27 on pilgrimage to Jerusalem and stayed on the continent for 50 years. After his father's death, Cuby was invited to return to Cornwall from the continent to rule his people. Baring-Gould conjectures that Cuby's return (aged 77) was after the rule had passed to Salamon's brother Cador and to Cador's son Constantine; that perhaps the offer to rule was in fact a request to head a rebellion against his unpopular cousin (if we are to believe the damning opinion of Constantine given by Gildas, Cuby's other cousin). Cuby declined the offer and Baring-Gould puts his hasty retreat to Gwynedd down to him fleeing for his life amidst a time of dynastic upheaval. This is of course all read between the lines as the definite line of kingship is unknown, but it makes for an interesting slant on the *Life*. It tells how Cuby was joined, amongst others, by his uncle **Cyngar**, who would have been of very advanced age if Cuby was 77![68] Besides the fact Cuby had no experience at ruling, it is likely he had no interest in spending the rest of his days festering on an earthly throne of men after spending his life striving to gaze on the throne of heaven.

We do not know if Cuby's Cornish sites of Duloe, and Cuby, near Tregony, were founded on this visit to Cornwall or in his early life before pilgrimage. Cuby went from Cornwall to Glamorgan, where Cyngar had supposedly founded the monastery of Llandough (detailed in his own *Life*, see below). This connection is not mentioned and the party were not received well by the local king but despite this Cuby was able to found two churches nearby: Llangybi-ar-Wysg and Llanddyfrwyr-yn-Edeligion, in modern day Monmouthshire.

He passed through Wales by way of another cousin, Saint David, before sailing to Ireland where it is said he spent the next four years. Cyngar was still with him at this time, and Cuby bought a cow to sustain his aged uncle with milk, since he could no longer manage solid food. He built a church at Arun but was subsequently driven from there after an altercation with another monk, Crubthir Fintan, who felt Cuby and his disciples were encroaching on his land. He went to settle in Meath but was pursued by the angry Fintan and driven from there also. The same happened at Magh Bregh, and Vobvun; Fintan not letting up his persecution until he had driven Cuby from Ireland. Upon their departure, Cuby placed a curse on Fintan that all his churches would be deserted and that his presence would be erased from the island.

Cuby made for Mona (Anglesey) but where he settled, Cyndab, was most probably Llangybi on the Lleyn peninsula. He came into dispute with the local king, Maelgwn of Gwynedd, who was another of the five kings criticised by Gildas. The trouble began when Cuby sheltered a goat that was being pursued by the king's dog but he managed to gain the king's assurance that he would not kill it. The *Life* mentions a further altercation between Cuby and Maelgwn but does not give details. This perhaps stemmed from the presence of Cuby's follower Caffo, who was a brother of Gildas and therefore would be unpopular with Maelgwn. The text is fragmentary but says that Cuby sent Caffo away from him, after which Caffo was murdered by men loyal to Maelgwn. Baring-Gould surmises that,

---

68 The reverend surmised that Cuby's other uncle, Just, also followed him to Gwynedd and Anglesey, accounting for his presence in these regions (Baring-Gould and Fisher, 1907 vol3: 294).

following this incident, the land that Cuby received on Anglesey from Maelgwn where he founded Caer Gybi (Holyhead), was a form of blood money (Baring-Gould and Fisher 1907 vol.2: 208). Built on an old Roman fort, Caer Gybi became an important monastery and later, secular church. Cuby died and was buried here circa 555.

Cyngar, we believe, made it all the way to Anglesey, following Cuby's trek across Wales and Ireland, as he has a church there at Llangyngar; or else it was dedicated by Cuby in his late uncle's name. We learn more about Cyngar from Cuby's *Life* than from Cyngar's own which is fragmentary and very low on information; full of saintly conventions such as reciting the Lord's Prayer while standing in cold water, and having a tree grow from where he planted his staff. Although we believe him to be a son of Geraint ab Erbin, the *Life* declares him to be son of an unnamed 'Emperor of Constantinople', this probably being due to his descent from Constantine Gorneu being mistaken for Constantine the Great. It tells how the Saxon king Ina granted him land at Congresbury in Somerset, which became a flourishing monastery[69]. After a time he allegedly left seeking solitude although Saxon incursion is a more likely motive. He crossed the Severn and founded Llandough in Wales "where he was called Docco", although it is more likely Docco was a separate saint so whether Cyngar was ever there is debatable. His Life was indeed written in South Wales, although probably for Wells Cathedral, which had claims to Congresbury (Orme 2000: 94). The only site associated with him in Cornwall is St. Ingunger, but its history is scarce and its link debatable[70].

Cuby's mother, **Wenna**, was sister to Saint **Non,** the mother of **David**, patron of Wales, making Cuby and David first cousins. She is represented as a queen as well as saint, and would have been wealthy enough to receive her sister Non and bequeath her land within Cornwall. Most of what we know about Non comes from the eleventh century *Life of St. David* by Bishop Rhigyfarch of St. David's. He tells how Non (rendered Nonnita in the original Latin text) was taken by force by Sandde (or Sant), prince of Ceredigion, but does not dwell on the violation; rather he concentrates on the miraculous foretellings of David's birth, which involved both Saint

---

69 This is an anachronism, as Ina was a king of the eighth century.

70 David Nash Ford believes the entire *Life of Cyngar* to be mistakenly attributed to Cyngar ap Geraint and that Congresbury was in fact founded by Cyngar ap Garthog ap Ceredig of Ceredigion (David Nash Ford 2005: 'EBK Cungar of Congresbury').

Patrick and Saint Gildas[71]. It is curious that David's parents are named 'Nun' and 'Saint', perhaps in order to emphasize his significance and holiness, despite the particulars of his conception[72]. His coming was so famed that a local ruler plotted to have the newborn killed, but was foiled by a massive storm; rain and lightning prevented anyone getting close to the place of birth where a bright holy light shone over Non. It is said she gripped a nearby stone so hard during labour that the impressions made by her fingers could thereafter be seen, the stone itself, cloven in two in sympathy with Non. On this spot a church was built and the stone set in the foundations of the altar. David was raised by Non at Henfeynyw near Aberaeron and she gives her name to Llannon nearby, where she is meant to have founded a convent.

At some point she travelled with her son to her sister's country of Cornwall where we have the parishes of Altarnun (literally 'Altar of Non') and Davidstow adjoining each other. Altarnun parish famously housed a chapel and well which was used for the curing of insanity through immersion, as reported by Carew in 1602, although its efficacy goes unmentioned. William of Worcester heard that Non was buried at Altarnun and David was born there. The former may be true, although her relics did not survive the Reformation; the latter is most likely untrue. Non is believed to have retired to Brittany and died and was buried at Dirinon near Brest, where there is an ornate tomb within her chapel. Similar to the tale of her labour pains, Dirinon holds a rock with impressions of her knees, where she knelt in prayer. Other dedications to Non include Pelynt and Grampound in Cornwall, and Bradstone in Devon although their association is late (eighteenth century) and less certain, based on the names Nynnina and Naunter who may well be separate saints (Orme 2000: 206). A holy well in Portscatho in the Roseland is supposedly dedicated to Non. Portscatho adjoins Gerrans and is postulated to be named after another son of Geraint, Cador.

Cador, unlike his brothers, appears to have no churches dedicated to him and it is unclear if he was ever regarded as a saint or merely as a ruler; inheriting Cornwall from his father Geraint. He

---

71 Another anachronism, as Gildas is generally believed to have been born after David.

72 It may be that the mother of David was an actual nun in the local monastery of Maucan or a virgin pupil when Sant took her, 'by divine inspiration'. It is held in the *Life* that she remained virgin thereafter whereas Irish sources claim David to have had siblings.

is mentioned as Cadwr, Earl of Cornwall in the *Dream of Rhonabwy,* and in another *Mabinogion* text, *Culhwch and Olwen,* there is mention of a Gadwy ap Geraint who may be Cador or else a separate sibling. The figure of Cador is used, somewhat creatively, by Geoffrey of Monmouth in his Arthurian pseudo-historical saga. He tells how Cador, Duke of Cornwall comes to Arthur's aid several times and does battle with the Saxons but any factual basis for this is unknown. Cador was confused with his brother Caw of Cwm Cawlwyd, in the *Iolo Manuscripts.*

Caw himself is quite a mysterious figure. Although he is mentioned in the genealogies as a son of Geraint, his kingdom is said to be in the North, in Prydyn (Pictland). How he came to be there we do not know but his descendants formed one of the famed 'great holy families' of the British Isles, like that of Brychan of Brycheiniog. His family were forced by Picts to flee to North Wales where we find a Llyn (lake) Cowlwyd in Snowdonia. Caw and his family were allowed to settle in Twr Celyn in Anglesey by Maelgwn, the king who had also granted Cuby and Cyngar land on Anglesey, as long as they promised to enter religious orders so as not to rival his secular power (Baring-Gould and Fisher 1907 vol.1: 36). Like Brychan, Caw was more of a patriarch than saint in his own right. Twenty-four sons are listed by the author of the *Life of Gildas* (arguably his most famous son) and twenty-one children are listed in *Culhwch and Olwen.*

Gildas, son of Caw, was perhaps renowned more as an author than a saint, his *De Excidio* influenced a wealth of medieval texts and is our primary source for him. Secondly we have two *Lives*; one written possibly as early as the ninth century or as late as the eleventh, by a monk of Rhuys, Brittany. The second *Life* from the twelfth century is attributed to Caradog of Llancarfan. Gildas himself writes that he was born in the year of the Battle of Mount Badon[73]. The Annales Cambriae places it at 516 but theories range from the 490s to 520s[74].

Gildas was sent by his father to study with Saint Illtyd at

---

73 Or rather 'siege of Mount Badon' as he describes it. This battle is traditionally claimed to be Arthur's twelfth and greatest victory against the Saxons before his final battle at Camlann. Gildas however does not mention Arthur by name in his record of the battle, only that the Britons were victors.

74 Baring-Gould believes Gildas to have been a young man of 30, not 15 when he entered Holy Orders, to take into account the period he would have fathered the 5 children given in the genealogies, Cenydd, Gwynog, Aidan, Nwython, and Dolgan (Baring-Gould and Fisher 1907 vol.3: 104-5).

Llantwit Major (see Chapter Six) at the age of fifteen, and Samson and Paul are mentioned as his fellows there[75]. He lived ascetically, existing on three meals a week. One of his early miracles claimed by the Rhuys Life was making the arid land around the monastery fertile through prayer, a story probably borrowed from the earlier *Lives* of Samson and Paul. The Caradog Life features a story also told in Rhigyfarch's Life of St.David in which Gildas, having returned from a seven year stay in Gaul, was preaching to a congregation when he was rendered dumb by some unseen force. Able to speak but not preach, he asked the congregation to go outside to see if the presence of one of them was affecting him, but none were. He called out again asking if anyone was hiding inside, to which the pregnant Nonnita replied from behind the door. He sent her outside until his sermon was finished and began to pray, receiving the message that his silence had been caused by the presence of one more blessed than any who had preached in that part of the country before, the unborn David. This story contradicts the view that Gildas was of the same age, if not younger than David[76].

Both *Lives* take Gildas to Ireland, the Rhuys *Life* having him receive blessing from Saint Brigid. Whilst in this version Gildas follows more saintly conventions such as visiting Rome and performing miracles, Caradog, influenced by Geoffrey of Monmouth and other contemporaries, adds more fantastical elements and stories involving King Arthur. Gildas' eldest brother Huail, a warrior, is mentioned. Rather than fleeing with the rest of his family to monastic life, Huail carried on fighting in his homeland and, according to the *Life*, making raids into Wales and refusing to recognise Arthur as king. Seeing him as a substantial threat to his throne, Arthur held a council of war on the Isle of Man and pursued and killed Huial[77]. Gildas returned from Ireland on hearing the

---

75 Baring-Gould believes Gildas to have been a young man of 30, not 15 when he entered Holy Orders, to take into account the period he would have fathered the 5 children given in the genealogies, Cenydd, Gwynog, Aidan, Nwython, and Dolgan (Baring-Gould and Fisher 1907 vol.3: 104-5).

76 Unless we follow Baring-Gould's model which calculates Gildas' birth to be in 476.

77 Welsh legend tells how Huail's death occurred because he and Arthur were duelling over the hand of a lady, and Huail wounded Arthur in the thigh, laming him. Huail was made to promise never to mention the fight again. Shortly after, Arthur met and fell for another lady, and disguised himself in female attire in order to get close to her. Huail recognised Arthur due to his dancing being hampered by his limp, and duly mocked him. Arthur did not take too kindly and had Huail beheaded on a stone called Maen Huail in

terrible news, but remaining true to his faith forgave and made peace with Arthur.

Whereas the Rhuys *Life* (predictably) makes more of Gildas' stay in Brittany, the Caradog *Life* speaks at length about Gildas' time at Glastonbury, which leads to suspicions that the manuscript may have some point been in the hands of, if not originated from, the monks of Glastonbury Abbey, keen to associate another famous saint with their foundation. It claims it was here he wrote his *De Excidio.* Gildas' coming to Glastonbury coincides again with an Arthurian episode; the abduction of Arthur's wife Gwenhwyfar by the rebellious king Melwas. His fort on Glastonbury Tor was besieged by Arthur; but with the help of Gildas, the abbot of Glastonbury was able to reinstate peace between the two kings. Gildas supposedly retired to nearby Street to live as a hermit and founded a church there. At the end of his life he requested burial in Glastonbury Abbey. This account may of course be entirely fictional, taking into account what we know about the Abbey in the twelfth century (see Chapter Four), and although the *Life* was written before the Great Fire of 1184 these details could still have been added at a later date. Far more tradition exists in Brittany for Gildas which points to it being a more likely candidate for where he ended his days. Some, however, believe the Gildas (Gueltas) of Rhuys and Gildas of Britain to be two disparate saints, despite the two *Lives* being in general agreement over most matters[78].

It is from Brittany that Gildas most likely wrote his work on the 'Ruin of Britain'. Far easier would it be to insult from a distance, and Gildas mentions nothing of the tyrants close at hand to him in Brittany. It would seem his complaints made life very difficult for members of his family in Wales including his sons who were living within regions ruled by the very kings upon whom he heaped venomous abuse. Gildas must have become extremely disillusioned with the secular by this time, to so openly insult the man, Maelgwn, who had granted his family a home in Gwynedd in his early years. Maelgwn he accuses of murdering his own uncle before taking, and breaking, Holy Orders, remarrying, and killing his wife and nephew! It is little wonder we find no dedications to Gildas in this region but must wonder at why he would so endanger his brethren in Anglesey

---

Ruthin.

78 Baring-Gould presents an interesting theory that the 'Gildas' buried at Glastonbury may be the foster son of the more famous Gildas who he named after himself on rescuing the child from being killed by a wicked Breton king, Conomor (1907 vol.3: 127).

including his cousins and brother Celyn and leave his own people so open to criticism. Was he perhaps angry that in the period of peace following the Battle of Mount Badon which subdued the Saxons, Britain had descended into civil wars amongst petty kings?

Gildas most famously railed against his own cousin **Constantine**, son of Cador of Cornwall. This king he described as the "tyrannical whelp of the unclean lioness of Damnonia"[79]. His estimated period of rule c.530-560 is contemporary to when Gildas would have been writing in the 540s. Gildas' explanation for his attack was, in addition to a gallery of wicked deeds, the alleged murder of two royal youths by Constantine; but more specifically because he had disguised himself as an abbot in order to gain access to the church where they claimed sanctuary and then had slain them on holy ground. Geoffrey of Monmouth expanded upon this story, once more drawing it into the Arthurian web, and making the two youths the sons of Mordred, who with the aid of the Saxons made insurrection against Constantine who was, according to Geoffrey, King Arthur's successor to the throne of all Britain. They fled to Winchester and London where Constantine found and killed them. Constantine was said to have converted to Christianity around 588 when he would have been an old man. This vow he kept, unlike the 'dreadful oath' he had previously made before God not to harm any of his subjects which Gildas accuses him of breaking.

The *Life of Petroc* gives the story of Constantine's conversion. Petroc one day saw a stag being hunted by men of Constantine and sheltered it. The hunters, being afraid to touch the beast under the holy man's protection, returned to their master who in a rage went to Petroc and would have attacked him with his sword, but immediately found his limbs frozen in his presence. When Petroc released him, Constantine submitted to him and became a follower of Christ. We cannot say for certain that this was Constantine, King of Dumnonia, as he is only referred to as a "wealthy man", but he left behind a church at St. Merryn near Constantine Bay, Padstow, and another in the parish of Constantine, near the area associated

79 The other kings attacked by Gildas, besides Maelgwn and Constantine, were Vortipor of Dyfed for murder and adultery, Cynglas of Rhos for defiling a nun, and Aurelias Caninus, a character we are unsure of the identity of but who he accuses of murder and general immorality. Despite coming from the same stock as these figures, Gildas shows little love or respect for his fellow Britons, even warrior queen Boudica, and his tone throughout appears to lament the end of the Roman regime.

with his Cornish royal antecedents. These churches were in existence at the time of the writing of Petroc's *Life* so Constantine's sainthood would have been already established. If the author was writing at Padstow and referring to the saint of the local church he may have been unaware he was a king, although in the seventeenth century at the other parish of Constantine, tradition remained that the saint had been a king, Nicholas Roscarrock records. Other parish churches of Constantine exist at Milton Abbot in Devon and Llangystennin in Wales, but these may well be dedicated to one of the numerous other Constantines, including the celebrated Emperor Constantine the Great or the Welsh Cystennin, son of Helen of Caernarvon, with whom he was often confused.

The *Life of St. David* tells how Constantine was said to have gone to the monastery at St. Davids after his conversion to atone for his sins, but this may have just been a way-station before moving on to Ireland where, it is told in the *Aberdeen Breviary,* a Cornish king lived in a monastery anonymously, grinding corn for seven years, until one day he was overheard commenting to himself about his noble birth, and was promptly made a priest. Following this he visited Saints Columba and Kentigern who made him an abbot and directed him to Galloway to preach. He was said to have died in Kintyre, maimed by marauders and left to bleed to death[80].

Returning to the matter of how Constantine came to be regarded by Geoffrey of Monmouth and others as the heir to Arthur's throne, we have already seen one way in which the families were thought to be linked. Geraint ab Erbin is mentioned as a cousin of Arthur in the *Mabinogion* possibly because both Erbin and Uther Pendragon were thought to be sons of Constantine Gorneu. However we are given another link through Arthur's mother Igraine. In the Welsh genealogies she is named Igerna ferch Amlawdd, who was sister to Geraint's wife Gwyar ferch Amlawdd, making Cador and Arthur first cousins and Constantine his second cousin[81]. Therefore Arthur's closest male relation after his death, assuming Cador had already died at this point, was Constantine. Gwyar is traditionally given in Welsh sources as the mother of Gwalchmai

80 The date the *Aberdeen Breviary* gives for Constantine's death is 576, earlier than the date other sources give for his conversion, which may be a mere inaccuracy, or confusion with a separate Constantine, perhaps Constantine of Strathclyde.

81 It was something of a literary trope to make someone's mother "a daughter of Amlawdd Wledig" in order to claim that figure's close kinship to Arthur and is used on various occasions in the genealogies and *Mabinogion.*

(Gawain) but this was later conferred to Anna/Morgause, sister of Arthur.

The Celtic tale of *Tristan and Iseult* is also linked to the families of Arthur and Geraint. In its standard form it features a love triangle between **Marc**, King of Cornwall, his nephew and foster son **Tristan**, and Marc's new wife, the Irish princess **Iseult**. Tristan, acting as Marc's champion, won Iseult for his uncle, but on the journey home from Ireland the pair accidentally drank a love potion intended for Iseult and Marc causing them to become lovers despite Iseult's impending marriage. The pair continued to meet in secret but were not as careful as they perhaps could have been and Tristan's enemies at court soon began to suspect their lovers' trysts. Marc's steward alerted him to his suspicions, and the king became increasingly preoccupied with catching the lovers out, trying to entrap Iseult with tests and questions that might belie her true feelings. Iseult agreed to undergo trial by hot iron at Arthur's court at Caerleon. She told Tristan in secret to disguise himself as a peasant and ferry her over the muddy riverbank at Caerleon on his shoulders. Thus, when questioned, she replied that the only men who had been between her legs were her husband and the peasant who had carried her. As her oath was technically not a lie she was saved from being burned by the hot iron.

Despite this episode, Marc still had anxieties and eventually exiled the pair from his home. Iseult was eventually reconciled with her husband but Tristan remained in exile, marrying a different Iseult, 'of the White Hands'. In the romantic version he is mortally wounded, and the ending sees him sending for the Irish Iseult to heal him, telling his steward to return with white sails if she is on board or black sails if she is not, but his jealous wife Iseult of the White Hands tells him falsely that the sails are black and Tristan dies of grief before Iseult can reach him.

The earliest literary mentions of Marc ap Meirchion, Tristan, and Iseult survive in the Welsh Triads and the *Mabinogion*, associating them with Arthur's court. The story's part in Arthurian saga was expanded and integrated at the height of its popularity in twelfth-century courtly romance. The historical truth around these personages, however, remains a mystery. Marc's father was Meirchion/Merion who was allegedly another son of Constantine Gorneu. It seems Constantine split his kingdom between his sons, Erbin inheriting Dumnonia and Merion taking the western part, Cerniw (Cornwall), perhaps separate to or under the overlordship of Erbin. Marc inherited Cornwall from his father and is mentioned in the *Life of Pol-de-Léon* as "Marcus Conomorus"[82]. Conomor may be translated as "Sea-hound", a title obtained perhaps through a confusion with Marc's great-grandfather, Cynfawr, which can be equated to the same meaning. Some scholars make Marc the son of Tewdrig, the tyrant king of West Cornwall, whilst others make him only Tewdrig's successor. He was generally an unpopular figure and was ridiculed by people saying he had ass's ears which he kept hidden under his hair which he grew long to cover them!

Tristan in legend is said to be the son of Rivalen and Blancheflor in early versions, and son of King Meliodas of Lyonesse[83] and Isabelle or Elizabeth in later versions. In most versions his mother is a sister of Marc. Marc's home was at Castle Dore, near Fowey, and nearby we have possibly the only piece of historical evidence for their existence. The 'Tristan stone' is an inscribed 7-foot-tall pillar with a cross on one side and on the other a Latin inscription that reads "Here lies Drustanus son of Conomorus"[84]. So either the legends were wrong and Drustan (the Latin form of Tristan) was in fact Marc's son, or they were right in the fact that a characteristic of all versions is the fatherly love Marc has for his nephew. The stone is dated to the latter part of the sixth century. Some scholars identify the Conomor of the stone with either Cynfawr, father of Custennin Gorneu, who was born back in the fourth century, far too early to match, or the Breton Conomor of Poher mentioned in the *Life of Gildas* and misidentified with Marc of Cornwall in the *Life of Pol-de-Léon.* Sixteenth century antiquarian Leland visited the stone and claimed to have seen an extra line, "with the Lady Ousilla" which some believe to be a Latin variation of Iseult. If the additional portion did exist it was probably lost on one of the several times the stone was moved.

The truth behind the highly hyperbolic figures of Tristan, Marc, and in particular Arthur, and their inclusion in the family tree of Constantine Gorneu may never be unravelled. What is certain is they add a layer of Arthurian mist over a family which, under

---

82 In the *Life,* Paul is invited to Marc's kingdom to preach Christianity and whilst there admires a particular bell belonging to Marc, but when Marc refuses to gift it to him, the pair fall out and Paul leaves, only to later discover the bell in the belly of a salmon.

83 A semi-mythical kingdom, variously theorised to be in Lothian, Brittany, or a region somewhere between Cornwall and the Scilly Isles, now lost beneath the waves.

84 Some archaeologists' interpretation of the inscription reads Cirusinlus/Cirusius due to the formation of the D, therefore perhaps invalidating the stone's link to the Tristan legend.

examination, was quite remarkable in its own right, blending royal and ecclesiastical power, for the most part successfully, over many generations.

Chapter 6

South Wales: Great School of the Saints

Saint David, as most people know, is the patron saint of Wales and holds the distinction of being the only British saint recognised by the Roman Catholic Church; but how did this come about, and what circumstances led to his foundation in South-West Wales receiving its prominent position? On examination we can see that St. David's was not always the principle religious site in Wales nor the eldest, but had its greatness accentuated by the Normans through their colonisation of the South-West, rebuilding of the cathedral, and especially through the influence of their authors and historians. St. David's had a rival, in the form of the See of Llandaff, in South Glamorgan, which also claimed primacy. They compiled charters in the *Book of Llandaff,* which also featured *Lives* of Dyfrig, Samson, Euddogwy, and Teilo to assert claim over churches within its territory, and set out through the use of the *Lives* to prove ownership over abandoned Dyfrig monasteries in Ergyng (between Hereford and Monmouth). Besides the two major religious centres of St. David's and Llandaff we have the monastic school of Llantwit Major, the cradle of early monasticism in Wales which produced many a renowned saint, including Gildas, Paul of Léon, Samson, and according to some, David himself. In examining these early Celtic foundations we can see a rich monastic heritage, the influence of which spread to Ireland, Cornwall, and Brittany.

Although David may be treated as "Wales' holiest Saint", **Illtyd** is often considered to be its greatest teacher. However, this could not have been predicted from his early years. The only surviving *Life of Illtyd* is twelfth century in composition and Arthurian in basis but arguably earlier than the *Historia* of Geoffrey of Monmouth as it appears uninfluenced by some of the more 'inventive' additions of Geoffrey, and as Arthur's importance in the story is relatively minor[85]. It tells how Illtyd was born in Armorica (Brittany) to Bicanus, a nobleman, and Rieingulid, daughter of Amlawdd Wledig, and had for aunts Gwyar, wife of Geraint ab Erbin (see Chapter 5) and Igerna, ie, Igraine, mother of Arthur[86]. His great uncle was Germanus of Armorica under whom he studied in his early life. Despite his upbringing and intelligence, Illtyd had no interest in monastic life and crossed to Britain to the land of his mother's people and took up a place in his cousin Arthur's warband. Indeed, one of Illtyd's epithets is Illtyd Farchog 'the Knight'[87]. It was during this time that he met his wife, Trynihid.

After some time he went to serve under Pawl of Penychen, King of Glamorgan. Pawl was brother of Gwynllyw and uncle of Cadoc, and treated his saintly nephew favourably. The story, as told in both the *Lives* of Illtyd and Cadoc, goes that Illtyd and a band of fifty of Pawl's men were out hunting one day and coming across Cadoc's lodgings, the men rudely demanded food of him for the entire party. Illtyd was absent, and was spared from what happened shortly after, the men being “swallowed up by the earth” - probably a marsh or bog – for their insolence. Illtyd returned to Cadoc, moved by his near-miss, and took his instruction to give up the knightly life for a monastic one.[88] He removed himself from Pawl's court, making camp near a river, Naduan, where he was visited in a dream by an angel who admonished his worldly ways, compounding Illtyd's resolve to enter Holy Orders. Illtyd rather harshly instructed his naked wife out into the night to see to the horses, and on her return refused to see or speak to her ever again! Following this he went to the next river, the Hodnant, and after gaining permission to

---

85 Some argue that Arthur's appearance shows Geoffrey's influence but the description of Dubricius (Dyfrig) as bishop of Llandaff as opposed to Archbishop of Caerleon is inconsistent with Geoffrey's work.

86 Doble notes that Illtyd's parents' names may well have been a later fabrication although allows that Rieingulid may genuinely translate to 'Gentle Maiden' (1971: 124).

87 First mentioned in the *Life of Cadoc*. It was perhaps due to the contemporary Norman military presence at Llantwit Major at the time of writing that Illtyd was retroactively made a knight (Doble 1971: 103).

88 This story is a fusion of two tales, the author of the twelfth century *Life of Illtyd* took an earlier story of Illtyd's men dying in a bog to be the same as the story about Cadoc, and how the men of Sawyl Benuchel suffered a similar fate, making Sawyl and Pawl one and the same. Therefore Cadoc (who may not have even have lived in his uncle's domain) became responsible for Illtyd's conversion. The tale was then copied from Illtyd's *Life* to Cadoc's, the author unwittingly duplicating the earlier incident. The whole event is a probable anachronism, as Cadoc would have been an infant at most at the time and was a contemporary of Illtyd’s pupils (Baring-Gould and Fisher 1907 vol.3: 306).

settle from Saint Dyfrig who saw to him being tonsured, Illtyd began building his church. It has been suggested that he took over an existing monastic school, Caerworgorn, but if there had been a previous site here, it was desolate and there was no continuation between it and the school of Llantwit Major.[89]

Sometime shortly after the founding of Llantwit Major, *Llanilltud Fawr* in Welsh, Illtyd came into contact with local king Meirchion[90]. The lord was out hunting, and in typical Saints' *Lives* style, pursued a fawn to the feet of Illtyd, where it sheltered from the hounds of the king. Meirchion agreed not to kill the fawn but was irritated at the saint for settling in the midst of his hunting grounds without seeking his permission. Illtyd refused to move but invited the king in for a meal, as he was hungry from the hunt. Initially unimpressed by the saint's plain fare of fish and water, Meirchion found that under Illtyd's command, the fish in his mouth tasted of many varied foods and the water tasted to him like wine and mead. Satisfied, he lay down for a nap, but was visited in a dream by an angel who lambasted him for his treatment of the saint and told him he should concede his grounds to him. On waking, Meirchion humbly confirmed that which had already been appointed to Illtyd by God and promised no further harassment to him[91].

Illtyd was able to continue unhindered in the creation of his monastery and laboured hard, building his settlement by hand, and with the help of the stag, which he had raised from a fawn. Local tradition says that when the burial place of 'Illtyd's Golden Stag' is found "great prosperity will come to Llantwit" (Baring-Gould and Fisher 1907 vol.3: 309). Illtyd is remembered not only for his learned ways but his skills in cultivation, and particularly for introducing a new method of ploughing to Wales. His hard work drew in many and it is said that at its height, Llantwit Major housed three thousand monks! Already mentioned are some of his pupils, Samson confirmed in the early *Life* of that saint from the seventh

---

89 The sixteenth century *Iolo Manuscripts* states Germanus of Auxerre appointed Illtyd to Caerworgorn but this is a mistake, probably stemming from Illtyd's pupillage under Germanus the Armorican.

90 Called 'Marc the Wild' or 'Marc the Mad'; not thought to be the same as the Cornish Marc (see Chapter 5), but sometimes confused with him, as the story of his having ass's ears has also been applied.

91 Doble considers the bulk of the story aside from the descriptions of Llantwit Major and its surrounds a figment, and the speeches of the angel and Meirchion too long drawn out to be convincing. The passage about Illtyd forsaking his wife is overlong and proselytizing, and tells more about the twelfth century monastic fear and repulsion of the female form (1971: 119-20).

century, which describes this 'Eltut' to whom Samson was sent, to be 'the most learned of all the Britons'. It has been suggested that the king Maelgwn Gwynedd was also sent there, as Gildas in his damning open letter to the Welsh princes (see Chapter 5) describes Maelgwn having been instructed by the most eloquent teacher of the Britons, however it does not explicitly name Illtyd[92].

Although Llantwit Major flourished, Illtyd had trouble with flooding and the sea wall he had constructed (or reconstructed from the Roman settlement of Bovium) was repaired and destroyed three times. Illtyd thought about abandoning the site but once again an angel intervened and told him to stand his ground. Illtyd was instructed to go to the shore, where the sea miraculously drew away from him, and after eliciting a spring with his staff, he drained the lands around the church so they were once again fertile for ploughing.

One day while he was working in the fields he was approached by his former wife, Trynihid, who had been searching for him. Despite her vow to remain chaste and devote her life to God she was punished for her curiosity to see her former husband and struck blind. Her sight was restored through Illtyd's prayers, but the saint would not speak with her and sent her away again, from whence she returned to her mountain dwelling and cared for nuns and widows and never saw Illtyd again.

Right: St. Illtyd: Icon of the knight-turned-scholar, Illtyd, who founded the monastic school of Llantwit Major. Here, he lays down his sword before a 9th-century cross which can today be found in the century local church, pictured in the distance. Acrylic and gold leaf on wood (9in x 12in).

92 This is the only text pointing to Maelgwn's schooling, none of the other saint's *Lives* mention him as a classmate, perhaps due to his secular standing and run-ins with various saints.

Illtyd retired to a cave retreat on the Ewenni river after Meirchion's steward made life difficult for him. The steward Cyflym was annoyed at Illtyd not paying taxes for the land he occupied. The *Life* tells how he exacted tributes from the clergy at Llantwit in Meirchion's name but before long was halted by God's wrath who made the man 'melt like candle wax'. Meirchion, unaware of his steward's wicked behaviour took offence at the death and, blaming Illtyd, planned to sack the monastery. Before this could happen, Illtyd removed himself to his refuge in the cave he had found, and remained there in secret for a year and three days. He was sent food from heaven to sustain him so he had no need to leave. Both his enemies and the people he had helped were perplexed, having no idea where he had gone. The many poor and needy he helped mourned his disappearance as he had been their only champion. Illtyd was only coaxed from his hideaway by the sound of a bell, which in legend commonly proved to be an irresistible item for a saint. A messenger was delivering said bell to Saint David as a present from Saint Gildas[93]. Illtyd was dismayed as he coveted the bell for his own after ringing it three times. On its arrival with David, the bell refused to sound, and the saint asked if it had been tested en route. The messenger told of Illtyd's delight in the bell and reluctance to ask for it and David at once declared that it should be sent to Illtyd as it was obviously destined for his hands. After delivering the bell, the messenger, stopping at Llantwit, told the monks where he had seen Illtyd and they rejoiced and sent for him to return. Illtyd decided it was safe as it could only have been by God's will that he had been found.

It was not long before Illtyd ran into trouble with the steward Cyflym's successor, Cefygid, who was more evil than the first. He frequently impounded and starved Llantwit's cattle but Illtyd still declined to curse him. Once again, matters were taken out of Illtyd's hands as Cefygid drowned in a bog at the Lord's vengeance. Meirchion himself shortly followed, as he once more came to attack Illtyd for the death of his steward. The author of the *Life* is careful not to implicate Illtyd in any way for these deaths but describes how he prays for his adversaries. Illtyd once again removed himself to a cave, this time at Llwynarth (Oystermouth, Swansea) where he stayed for three years.

It was here that a curious episode occurred. Illtyd was praying

93 Presumably both saints were grown and settled in their own foundations at this point, otherwise an anachronism.

in his sea cave when a ship approached bearing two men with the body of another who was described as a most holy man. Above the body was a portable altar, floating in mid air which followed the body wherever it was taken. The men bade Illtyd bury the man but would not reveal his name 'lest men come to swear oaths upon his grave', a practice surviving from early Christianity. Some believe that this man was Arthur, and he had been brought for burial by his cousin. The story is taken from the ninth century 'Marvels of Britain' by Nennius which adds extra information not transferred into the *Life of Illtyd.* The saint built a church around the grave, over which the altar continued to levitate. One king came to test the miracle by passing a staff beneath it but was struck dead shortly after. Another who tried to look beneath it became blinded and also died within a month.

The *Life* tells how Illtyd desired to see Mont St. Michel, where the archangel had appeared but this is of course an anachronism as the apparition did not happen until the early eighth century. He had heard about a famine in Brittany so set sail with ships filled with grain from Llantwit's abundant stores. His actual reason for visiting Brittany, as suggested by Baring-Gould, is that many other houses were colonising there from Britain and Illtyd was looking for viable land for daughter-houses for Llantwit (1907 vol.3: 312). He probably landed in Aber-Ildut where he founded the church of Llanildut, before travelling through Cournouaille. He was received joyfully and the people desired Illtyd to stay with them, but instead he returned to Britain. However it is said he returned to Brittany when his time approached and died and was buried at Dol. This might suggest the author had access to the early *Life of Samson* which was written in Pental for Dol, as a cleric of Llantwit would surely otherwise have taken the saint to have been buried at his own foundation, but its story of Illtyd's death does not mention his resting place, neither does the later *Life of Samson.* It tells how on his death-bed Illtyd called two abbots to him, and prophesied that at his hour of death, the abbot Isanus would see Illtyd's soul leave his body on golden eagle's wings and at the same time see the other abbot Atoclius' soul depart him but on heavy leaden wings, due to his avarice, and that Isanus would follow them into death forty days later, all of which came to pass. This episode and its figures are completely missing from the *Life of Illtyd* as are several other tales. There may have been another *Life of Illtyd* written after that of Samson but now extinct, from which the Llantwit author may have been taking his traditions, as well as the author of Saint Pol de Léon's *Life* which features similarities. Mentions of Samson in our surviving *Life of*

Illtyd do not correspond with those in his own *Life* and probably serve to explain the appearance of the name Samson three times on the ancient Celtic crosses that survive to this day at Llantwit Major, now displayed in its refurbished Galilee Chapel. However if these stones are indeed funerary monuments the dating of them is a couple of centuries late to refer to Samson the saint, but rather an abbot of the ninth century named after him.

The *Life* of **Samson** is of early composition, and was said to have been related to the author by someone who had been in a monastic house of Samson for eighty years and was told stories by his uncle Enoch, a deacon who was a cousin of Samson, who in turn had been told stories by Samson's mother, Anna. A layer of embellishment may still lie on the facts but compared to many saints' *Lives* that are often composed centuries after their lifetime, this is relatively contemporary, maybe forty or fifty years after Samson's death (Baring-Gould and Fisher 1907 vol.4: 131-2). Of course many marvels are attributed to Samson in the *Life* but this is the standard format for such a document, and we should remember not to view it as a historical account despite the proximity between the time of creation and the events in the story[94].

The *Life* paints Samson as a rather jolly and witty man, fond of foxing people by speaking in riddles. This early *Life* is replete with mystical encounters, including witches, serpents and spirits, remnants of an earlier age. Later legends recorded in the *Iolo Manuscripts* make Samson the grandson of Uther Pendragon and half brother of Saint David but this rests on the theory of his mother Anna (daughter of Meurig ap Tewdrig) being one and the same with the Anna of Arthurian legend. It also records he was Archbishop at York, Bishop of St. David's and buried at St.Illtyd's but these are all other Samsons[95].

Early in his life Samson was sent to the monastery of Saint Illtyd - who had baptised Samson after the name of the great judge of Israel. He is described as being an astute student, even confidently entering into religious debates with his mentor. He

94 A second, later *Life* uses anecdotes found in the previous one and also events taken presumably from an earlier common source, but orders them more chronologically.

95 The reason for this appears to be to support the claims of Dol and St David's to be metropolitan sees (Baring-Gould and Fisher 1907 vol.4: 139).

Above: St. Samson: This painting shows St. Samson of Dol in an uncharted land of dragons, witches, and pagan monoliths, as told in the early 'Life of Samson'. Acrylic on canvas (15.5in x 15.5in).

began fasting at the age of fifteen, but Illtyd forbade this strain on his still growing body. His *Life* tells how Dyfrig visited one Sunday to ordain two priests and one deacon. As Dyfrig was choosing his deacon, a dove flew in and alighted on Samson's shoulder, proving him to be the chosen candidate, a motif that is repeated when Samson is made priest and bishop.

The favouritism accorded to Samson earned him enemies in the form of his cousins, two nephews of Illtyd who were concerned that Samson would potentially be made abbot on Illtyd's death rather than one of them. The pair tried to poison him with a herb infusion but were unsuccessful. Still, Samson was aware of his unpopularity amongst his brethren and removed himself to Caldey Island, which was known as Ynys Pyr for its abbot, Pyr[96]. Samson was welcomed at the monastery and re-entered the monastic life with even greater fervour than before.

Messengers arrived one day from his father, Amon of Dyfed who was ill and feared he would die, but refused communion from any other than his son Samson. He was reluctant to leave the monastery but Pyr encouraged him to go. Whilst journeying with a young deacon a curious episode took place. From out of the forest they were confronted by an old woman who is described as having wild grey hair and wielding a spear which she launched at Samson's young companion. The spear missed the boy but he promptly fainted and could not be roused by Samson. He bade the woman not to move and demanded she tell him who she was. She told him she was one of the original inhabitants of the land, a heathen, and is thus interpreted by some as being a witch. Samson commanded she revive the deacon but she could not, so in anger Samson cursed her and she fell down dead. Baring-Gould surmises that due to the detail the story goes into, the young companion may have actually been the deacon, Enoch (1907 vol.4: 144-5). Samson was later questioned by Dyfrig whether he struck the woman or if she fell dead at his curse alone, as there was fear that her people were powerful necromancers who would avenge a physical attack, yet strangely it implies killing someone with words alone was justifiable. The power of words here is one of the curious crossovers from the druidic to the Christian. Presumably a curse drew on a higher power than that which could be summoned by the necromancers and its usage was acceptable over physical violence.

On the attendance of Samson, Amon vowed to devote himself to God and at his wife Anna's request, entrusted his five younger sons into Samson's care. They had a sister also but Samson refused to

96 Terry Breverton prefers Barry Island as the site of Pyr's abbey, not Caldey, due to its proximity to Llantwit Major and association with both Samson and Dyfrig who were based in the South-east of Wales (2000: 465-6). Although it is possible, as monasteries named 'Ynys' were not always a literal but sometimes a spiritual island, this view challenges accepted opinion that he was based at Caldey.

take her as he regarded her as selfish and vain. Samson took his brothers, and also his parents, and aunt and uncle into religious orders and they travelled with him to Ynys Pyr to give up their worldly goods. In the description of their journey we find another curious pre-Christian motif when they are confronted with a great snake which reared up to attack them. Samson fearlessly advanced on the snake, and in terror it ate itself, swallowing its own tail[97].

On their arrival back at Ynys Pyr, Samson and company found Dyfrig in attendance, as he spent the period of Lent there. During his stay, the abbot Pyr, who was known to be a drunkard, stumbled into a well in a haze one night and died. Dyfrig called a council and declared Samson the new abbot. It soon became clear that Pyr had been an ineffective and lazy abbot, emphasized perhaps to highlight the hard-working Samson who immediately set reforms in motion. The monks did not relish the new strict regime and eventually their non-compliance drove Samson to visit Ireland, leaving his father and uncle in his place.

Whilst in Ireland, Samson was asked to exorcise an evil spirit from an abbot, by the monks of an abbey who had been forced to chain their master. Samson cast out the spirit and removed the abbot, sending his own uncle to take his place when he returned to Ynys Pyr. He did not reclaim his place as leader of the monastery on his return but took a small ragtag band which included his father, the Irish abbot, the cousin who attempted to take his life, and another, perhaps the deacon Enoch, to retreat from the world. They found a deserted area along the Pembroke coast, now known as Stackpole to base their camp. They were however not here long before Dyfrig recalled Samson and appointed him temporary abbot over Llantwit Major. This episode in the *Life* appears to coincide with the absence of Illtyd from his monastery at the time he was being persecuted by the spiteful steward.

On Illtyd's return, Samson coincidentally received divine inspiration to visit Brittany. This very restless saint first paid visit to the churches set up by his mother and aunt in Gwent and whilst there, excommunicated his sister for daring to marry rather than

---

97 The Ouroboros, the symbol of a snake eating its tail, is an ancient emblem usually signifying eternity or cycles of renewal. It is a prevalent symbol throughout the world, in medieval times known best as the serpent Jormungund in Norse mythology that encircled the world and held its own tail in its mouth. Although little used in Christianity, it may be that in this case it depicted the limits and confines of the material world, a 'vicious circle' which was overcome by Samson's spirituality.

follow the family into monastic life (despite refusing the opportunity to take her on himself at their father's house). The *Life* describes how after a voyage by ship he came to the monastery of Dochau. This, rather than being the foundation at Llandough, Cardiff, which would not require such a voyage, is likely to have been the Cornish settlement of Docwin (modern day St. Kew), near Padstow, which was a popular crossing place for travellers passing over to the continent from Wales or Ireland. Samson hoped to be gratefully received but the abbot Winiau bade him not stay there, although he requested he prove his saintliness with a miracle, a practice well known today but not a requirement of sainthood in those days.

Many sites across Cornwall mark Samson's overland part of the journey, beginning with the position of his chapel overlooking Padstow[98]. In a rickety, heavily laden wagon, Samson and his company ventured northeast along the old Roman road in the direction of the settlement of Laneast. Near here Samson once again encountered native pagan practices at a standing stone on a hill where a scene of revelry and dancing was taking place. The merry-makers protested their innocence and right to their customs but Samson was angered by their 'devil-worship' and lambasted the gathering. A young boy, a noble of the tribe, who was galloping around the group on a horse was thrown off and knocked out. Samson went to the boy and revived him through prayer. The mystified tribe were now willing to listen to Samson and agreed to halt their revelry, for that year at least. Samson supposedly engraved a cross on the top of the menhir, re-appropriating the pagan monument into a Christian one[99]. In the first *Life,* Samson later discovers the revellers were all baptised Christians, who were only acting out old customs without religious significance, much the way May-pole dancing persisted in folk tradition down the centuries. The later *Life* has them converted from paganism by Samson to emphasize his holiness.

After this episode Samson was called to slay another serpent. Suggestions of what the motif of the snake or dragon in the *Life* of a

---

98 His cult was definitely established there by the eleventh century when the author of the *Life of Petroc* wrote that Samson occupied the area before Petroc's coming (Orme 2000: 229).

99 This cross still survives although not in its original position. Samson was apparently fond of incising crosses into standing stones, other stones named for Samson stand in Dol and variously throughout Wales. (Breverton 2000: 465) Three Celtic crosses stand in St Illtyd's newly restored Galilee Chapel, one dedicated to Samson and one accredited to a Samson, celebrating Illtyd and Samuel, although this may be the later bishop of the same name.

saint represented include a secular tyrant or perhaps even a pagan wicker sacrificial structure which was used to burn offerings (Baring-Gould and Fisher 1907 vol.4: 158). Samson muzzled the 'beast' with his girdle and threw it into the nearest river, the Lynher. On the site of the serpent's cave he elicited a spring and founded the monastery of South Hill. The truth of the story may be that Samson subdued a local tyrant and coerced money and land from him to build a new religious foundation.

Whatever the case, Samson was obviously in no rush to get to his destination of Brittany as he appeared to spend a long time in Cornwall, extending his presence down to Golant, reputed to be where King Mark and the fair Iseult came to pray, and from here spreading his followers to found new monasteries thereabouts. Samson possibly had a chapel on the isle amongst the Scillies which bears his name although no trace remains. Once satisfied with the progress made in the relatively un-Christianised region of Cornwall, Samson gathered his disciples to make the crossing to Armorica, leaving his father to govern at South Hill. They landed at Guioult at the port of Winniau, possibly named after the same Winiau who had met them at Padstow and presumably gone ahead to the continent.

Samson settled at Dol, as far as possible from the native tyrant Conomor who was not fond of saints. The *Life of Teilo* tells us that Samson was settled here before the outbreak of the Yellow Plague, during which Teilo fled Britain and took refuge with his fellow. As Samson's power and influence grew, he sent messengers to try to gather support to overthrow the usurper Conomor, accusing the Domnonian regent of murdering his king, Jonas, in order to steal his throne. Samson sought to place Jonas' son Judwal at the head of the revolution but he was a prisoner of the king, Childebert, in Paris, who had no problem with Conomor and refused to give up his captive.

Samson's *Life* tells us he made an enemy of the Queen when he threatened her and the King, and for a second time in his life, an attempt was made to serve him poison. Samson, however, made the sign of the cross over the vessel he was offered which burst and scorched the hands of the page[100]. The biographer intimates that the Queen Ultrogotha was in love with the young prince Judwal and

100 A happening no doubt inspired by a similar event in the *Life of St Martin,* a most famous saint whose miracles were influential to the breadth of Celtic hagiography.

did not want to see him leave so planned to poison Samson and her husband. The next day Samson was given a horse by the Queen which bucked and threw the saint. Samson accused the Queen of once again trying to orchestrate his death by giving him a wild horse. It is even claimed that she set a lion on him! As Samson was at the altar, Ultrogotha turned her back on him and for this final insolence was rewarded with a gory death, her eyes falling from her head and blood pouring from the sockets until she expired[101].

To pacify Samson, Childebert offered him land at Pental, Normandy which became St. Samson-sur-Rille, and again the motif of Samson ridding the region of a serpent is used. He was, however, not pacified by the King's gift and continued his petition to free Judwal, and eventually succeeded. Besides freeing Judwal, the king endowed Samson with land at Rimou, and awarded the Channel Islands to him also, where Judwal's army were trained. It is told that in an effort to root out paganism there, Samson bribed the young people with a gold coin each not to celebrate the 'heathen' festival of New Years Day.

The motives of saints that became embroiled in political disagreements may not have always been as entirely righteous as one might think, and it is known that Judwal was a cousin of Samson and if he was restored to his throne, Samson's monasteries could have expected great financial reward. This is exactly how events ensued, with Judwal defeating Conomor in battle and Samson returning to Dol with rich rewards. Samson once more returned to Paris, meeting Germanus while he was there and attending a council of bishops in 562, not long before his death in 565.

The story of how Samson grounded a flock of birds that were marauding his cornfields and drove them into a barn as if they were sheep is told here in the late stages of his life. It is a familiar tale, as in the *Life* written for the Book of Llandaff circa 1150 it was transplanted into his childhood years at Llantwit Major and thus repeated in the *Lives* of Illtyd and Paul, although the latter makes Paul the hero of the story. Whereas the Book of Llandaff features a comparatively 'late' *Life of Samson*, it is our earliest source for the *Life of Teilo*. The *Life* of **Teilo** begins by telling us the interesting fact that his name derives from 'Elios' or Helios, the Greek name for,

---

101 The author shows a strong bias against Ultrogotha, who according to Gregory of Tours was actually a pious woman who outlived her husband (Baring-Gould and Fisher 1907 vol.4: 164).

and deity of, the sun, because his intelligence shone as brightly. Mention is made that Teilo began his education under Dyfrig but no detail is given. He was sent to Paulinus, who was teaching at Ty Gwyn, the foundation in South-west Wales where St. David was also receiving his education. When David left to set up his own school of Glyn Rhosyn, Teilo accompanied his friend. Many events of Teilo's *Life* are dependent on the *Life of David* although the details are changed to give Teilo the spotlight, such as when the friends travel to Jerusalem alongside Padarn. In this version, Teilo chooses correctly from three thrones, picking the wooden over the metal, showing that he is the most humble and like Christ[102]. They each receive a gift, Teilo receiving a bell. In the version of the story told in the *Life of St. David*, the titular saint is of course the sole recipient of all the gifts. The story, which was probably mere fabrication, would have originated from David's *Life* as a means of proving St. Davids' independence from Canterbury by showing approval from Jerusalem. The version in the *Life of Teilo* with its alterations was written at Llandaff to prove Teilo's dominance at a time when Llandaff was laying claim to Teilo churches in David's see.

Whereas Teilo may have been consecrated bishop of Llandaff, the title of 'archbishop' later applied to him did not exist in the modern sense, and it cannot be claimed he had any authority over the abbeys of Llancarfan, Llantwit, and Llandough. Neither did he hold sway in the See of St. Davids despite having a church there[103]. Its presence there was merely due to the inheritance of land in the region from his family. Despite the heated rivalry between the two diocese in the twelfth century, in Teilo's time this structure simply did not exist. Teilo did however make great progress and expansion for Llandaff in his time as bishop, with 37 churches dedicated to him across South Wales. It was he, rather than Dyfrig who was the original patron of Llandaff, his name being synonymous with it in all aspects – its bishops were called 'Esgob Teilo', its church 'Eglwys Teilo', even the *Book of Llandaff* 'Llyfr Teilo' (Baring-Gould and Fisher 1907 vol.4: 232).

In 547 came the Yellow Plague. As mentioned earlier, Teilo set out to visit Samson at Dol, passing through Cornwall and the territory of King Gerran (see Chapter 5). Whilst in Brittany he visited his brother-in-law King Budic, who it is pretended offered

---

102 Teilo taking the equivalent position in the Celtic church of St Peter whilst David equalled St James (Baring-Gould and Fisher 1907 vol.4: 230).
103 Gerald of Wales mistakenly wrote that Teilo succeeded Cenauc, the successor of David, a clear anachronism.

him primacy over all Armorica. He had no such power to invest Teilo, although he did endow him with territories in Cornouaille and surrendered to him his son Oudoceus (Euddogwy) for his teachings.

Teilo is associated with horses, being allegedly sent a horse from heaven, and blessing the men of Armorica to be excellent horsemen, seven times better on horseback than on foot. Seven years and seven months later, after the restoration of Judwal to power by Samson, Teilo left Brittany. He passed back through Cornwall, fulfilling his promise to Gerran, and returned to Llandaff.

In 577, after the Battle of Deorham in Gloucestershire, the Saxons began to make incursions into Wales. Iddon, son of the King of Gwent stood against them and was aided by Teilo, who took a role reminiscent of the druids of ancient times, standing on a hill and hurling curses at the foes of the British. Teilo's prayers for victory and cursing of their enemies apparently won them the battle, and Iddon rewarded Teilo with a church built on the site. The *Life* shows Teilo as influential with several kings, gaining land from them through favours or as recompense for their wrong-doings.

Teilo died at Llandeilo Fawr in Carmarthenshire and the legend goes that as Llandeilo wanted to keep his body as did Penally, the place of his birth, and Llandaff, his principal site, Teilo's corpse satisfied their claims by multiplying into three. This legend was obviously retroactively applied to explain the claims of all three churches that they housed his body. Baring-Gould shrewdly points out that it is likely that if Llandaff, who commissioned this hagiography, had truly possessed his relics then they would not have bothered to promote such a story (1907 vol.4: 237).

As mentioned, many Teilo sites exist across South Wales, and more still are now extinct. The stepping stones across the River Ewenny by Ogmore Castle were mistakenly labelled the 'Stepsau Teilo' but his actual stepping stones crossed the River Ogmore and no longer remain. The church of Llandeilo, the site of Teilo's death, claimed to house a piece of his skull, which was used as a bowl to drink the water from his holy well to impart good health. The family who guarded the relic claimed to descend from a maid who attended Teilo on his death bed and was instructed by the saint to remove his skull from his tomb a year after his death for this purpose. Even after examinations suggested the surviving piece came from the skull of a young person, not an aged man, people still made the pilgrimage to drink from it. It was sold in the twentieth century and for a time went missing, but it eventually found its way back to the cathedral of Llandaff where it is now in safe keeping. Other remembrances of Teilo abound in Brittany including stone chairs, dolmens, and sarcophagi. Britain had his silver relics but these did not survive the Dissolution.

We come now to **David**, whose birth to parents Non and Sant is described in Chapter 5. Details of his schooling are contradictory in various *Lives*. No trace of 'The Old Bush' where he is said to have began his studies remains. David's first biographer Rhygyfarch's *Life* agrees with Teilo's, saying that David went to the Ty Gwyn with Teilo under Paulinus. Yet Paul of Leon's *Life* said Paul was schooled under Illtyd alongside David, Gildas, and Samson. Gildas' *Life* does not mention David's education.

David is claimed to have founded twelve monasteries across Britain, including Glastonbury, and cleansed and heated the geothermal springs of Bath (which were in fact in use from at least Roman times). Many of those listed in England and Scotland did not in fact have anything to do with David, including Leominster, Coldingham and Repton, and would have been in the lands of the Angles and Saxons. It is said he then returned to the Old Bush and took over around 526 but was shortly after confronted by Gildas who sought to absorb the monastery under his own foundation. David had the better claim, the Old Bush being founded by his grandfather Cynyr. Cadoc was called to intervene in the matter but refused to take sides, leaving the decision to his pupil Finnian of Clonard, who pronounced in favour of David. The story which Rhygyfarch records of Gildas being struck mute in the unborn saint's presence is adapted from the *Life* of Saint Ailbe (Elvis), the bishop who baptised David. The reason perhaps was to show Gildas as subordinate to David to counter the claims Gildas made over David's see. It is also possible Gildas turned out the shamed and pregnant Non from the church, but in later years when Non and David's sainthood grew, the story had to be changed (Baring-Gould and Fisher 1907 vol.2: 290-1).

At some point it occurred to David that his seat at the Old Bush was relatively vulnerable to attack, easily accessible from the sea by pirates and pillagers. David decided to give up the site and with his disciples including Teilo, moved further inland. The territory of Glyn Rhosyn which David chose was near the settlement of a Goidelic invader and druid, Boia. The story goes that Boia was coerced by his wife into investigating the newcomers in his territory and sent out troops, but finding themselves unable to attack, they blasphemed against God and David, causing their cattle to drop dead. Boia, realising his mistake, repented and allowed the monks to stay, and had his cattle restored to life by David. Boia's wife was infuriated by her husband's decision so took matters into her own hands. She sent her handmaidens to bathe and play provocatively in the stream near the monks who understandably complained at this display of temptation; but David commanded them to ignore them and the women would soon give up this ploy. Further incensed, Boia's wife resorted to black magic and sacrifice to try to remove David from the locality, luring her step daughter into the forest and spilling her blood for the old gods. Her sacrifice failed and Boia's wife fled. In the meantime, Irish pirates led by an enemy of Boia invaded and slew the leader and burned his hall. The spot where Boia's daughter's blood flowed out elicited a spring, despite the girl being unbaptized.

Peace followed and David was free to build his monastery, receiving saintly students from near and far. This section of the *Life* gives us detail of the monks' daily practices, which under David, similarly to Samson, were disciplined and labour-intensive, and likely not tolerable to all. At one point an attempt was made on David's life by a disgruntled deacon, in league with a prior and cellarer. David's disciple Aidan, who had removed himself to Ireland, was warned by an angel of the murder plot, so sent Saint Scuthin, who was borne across the Irish sea in record time, to foil the plot which was to be carried out the next day.

Right: St. David: Here, David, the patron of Wales is shown in his early life, an enthusiastic evangelist, full of youthful optimism. He is accompanied by his dove and beloved bell or 'Bangu', and the aqua-colour signifies his epithet Dyfrwr – 'The Waterman'. Acrylic and gold leaf on wood (8in x 12in).

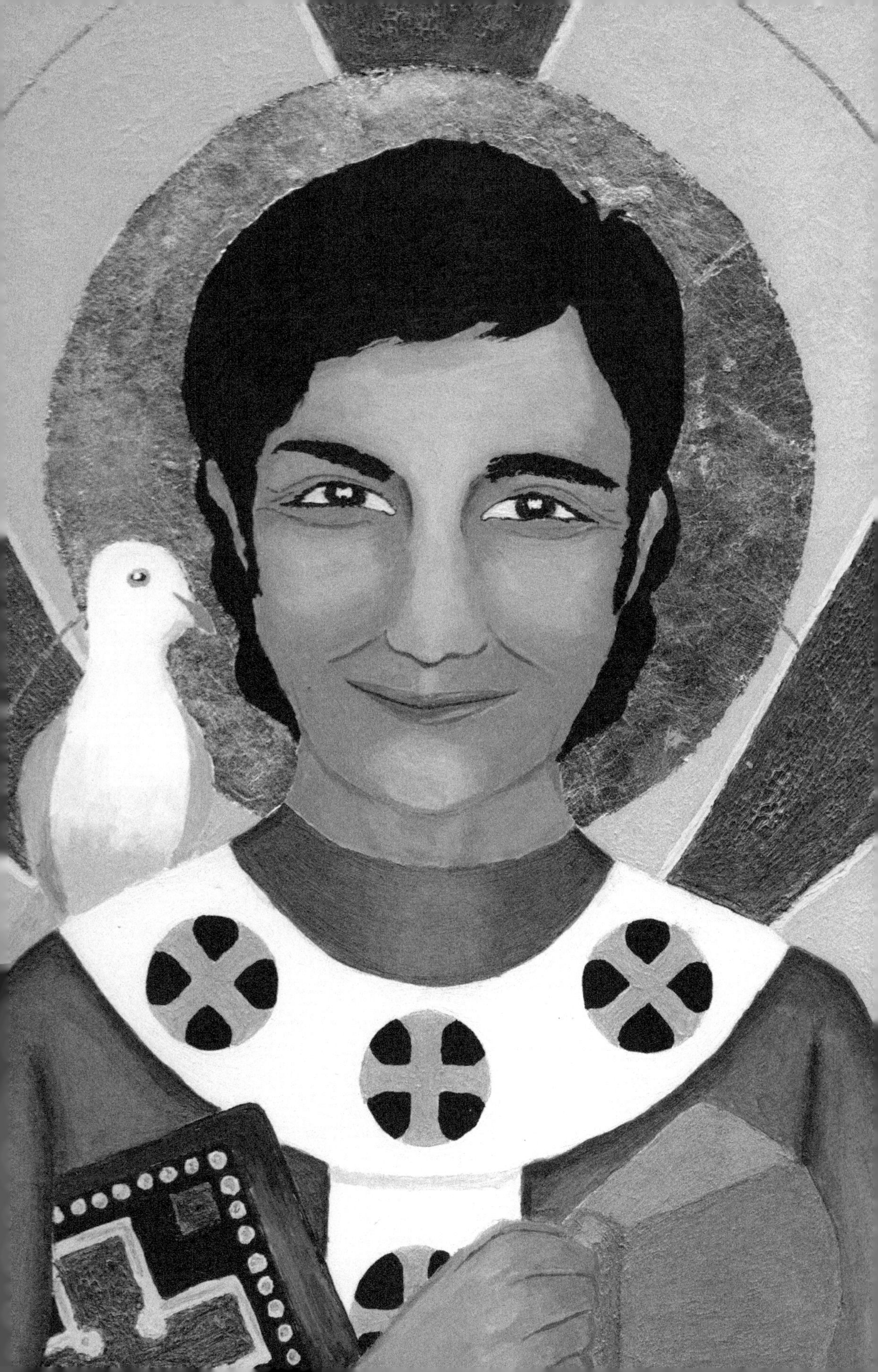

Happier occurrences of daily life at the monastery are told, as another disciple, Modomnoc, who had been bee-keeper, on quitting Glyn Rhosyn was followed by the bees who alighted on his ship. Modomnoc piously returned the swarm but as he attempted to leave, the bees again followed. David gave Modomnoc his blessing to take the bees thither to Ireland and the *Life* relates that this was the beginning of the tradition of bee-keeping, and indeed the first appearance of bees in the island. However, as we have seen previously, not all of these Celtic holy men were placid and docile. The *Life* of another Irish visitor, Molacca, tells us how on his trip to Glyn Rhosyn he knocked out and killed a young page in anger, his defence being that the boy had been impertinent. David still had just cause to be angry and for this and other crimes was forced to introduce a Penitential Code.

David was loathe to involve himself in matters outside of his own church and refused three times the invitation sent by his former teacher Paulinus to attend the synod of bishops held c.545 to discuss canons of discipline and the Pelagian Heresy, a movement started by the Briton Pelagius based on the belief in free will and denial of original sin. His views were dangerous to the Church as they effectively suggested that man could reach heaven through his own efforts, negating the need for the intercession of the ecclesiastical hierarchy. No conclusion had been reached at the meeting, and the bishops were desperate for one whose preaching could unite the gathering. Finally Dyfrig and Daniel went to David and he eventually agreed to attend, which indicates the respect awarded these two saints. The story goes that David ascended a mound that miraculously swelled under his feet and from its height he was able to address the entire gathering and gained their admiration. The site of the meeting is now called Llanddewi Brefi. The *Life* suggests that it was at this point that David was awarded the sovereignty over all the saints of the British Isles and St. Davids became a metropolitan see.

Although given in the *Life* before the Council of Brefi, David probably went abroad from Wales with his compatriots shortly afterwards, when the Yellow Plague broke out. His *Life* records the story of the trip to Jerusalem repeated in the *Lives* of Teilo and Padarn but of course making David chief amongst them. It is likely this journey never actually took place but that he did leave Menevia at some point. We can attest that his travels took him through Cornwall to Armorica, most likely collecting his mother Non en route, as they both have cults in these places. It has been suggested the residence he took in Leon may be the reason David was later confusingly labelled the Archbishop of Caerleon by Geoffrey of Monmouth and later by Gerald of Wales, an imaginary position inherited from Dyfrig in Geoffrey's works (Baring-Gould and Fisher 1907 vol2: 304).

On returning to Britain, David settled many parish churches and there was much crossover in areas settled by his friend Teilo. 42 churches now stand in the see of St. Davids, eight belong to Llandaff and three are in Hereford. As mentioned, there was no diocese established by David, and he and Teilo worked harmoniously, unaware that the boundaries of their territories would be under contention in the days of their biographers.

In Rhygyfarch's original *Life,* David is said to have attained 147 years before he left this world, a generous estimation! On perceiving that he was dying, David kept a vigil for several days in the church and preached a Sunday mass, remaining there until Tuesday 1st March when he was lifted to heaven with much fanfare, as witnessed by the many saints and people of the land who had come to mourn his passing. The year of his death varies wildly, the most popular estimate being 589, based on varying factors including the dates of other saints' deaths. David's canonisation did not occur until the twelfth century and it was at this time that his pre-eminence above the other saints of Wales occurred and he came to be regarded as patron saint. He remains the only Welsh saint ever to have been formally recognised by the Roman Church. Breverton argues that David overtook Gwenfrewi (Winifred, see Chapter 7) in popularity in Wales, only when her relics were removed to Shrewsbury and, had they not, her cult might have grown enough in prominence for her to overshadow David and be named patron (2000: 199).

One of David's epithets was 'The Waterman' as he and his monks lived an ascetic lifestyle, eating simple foods and drinking only water. Similarly to Samson, David is often represented with a dove around him. The origins of his association with the leek, which became the Welsh national emblem are uncertain but are likely to be relatively modern as none of the stories about David involve leeks, or daffodils for that matter, his other emblem. The leek in the history of Wales is a sign of victory in battle and was actually linked by Shakespeare with St. David's Day.

In medieval times other legends about David, unmentioned in his *Lives,* sprang up including one in which he turned two men and their mother who had been made wolves for their sins back into human form, perhaps signifying outlaws purified by David. Corpse candles were also associated with David and other Welsh saints. These were ghostly phenomena usually in the form of floating candle flames that proceeded from a house to a graveyard, thought to signal a death in the home and the route their funeral would take, alighting on the place of burial. It is thought the appearance of these corpse lights came through the Prayer of St. David, a sign from God about the existence of the afterlife.

His relics were kept in his church in a portable shrine which was stolen in the eleventh century. In the following century Glastonbury Abbey claimed to have his remains and that they had been transferred there in the tenth, although in 1173 King Henry II was said to have witnessed them in their original position in St. Davids. Further, more elaborate, shrines followed within the Cathedral, and were the focus of many royal pilgrimages throughout the Middle Ages.

Another saint who was set up in 'opposition' to David was **Cadoc** of Llancarfan. Besides David and Teilo, (and in North Wales, Beuno and Winifred) Cadoc was one of the prime contenders to be considered patron of Wales and was actually favoured over David by the Normans. The monastery of Llancarfan in Glamorgan used Cadoc's *Life* to not only emphasize Cadoc's superior holiness, but to actually denigrate David by insinuating he called the Synod of Brefi himself for his own glorification, despite David admitting 'in his own words' in the text that Cadoc was wiser and more worthy of assembling a synod. The *Life* is the longest and most extant of any of the Celtic saints, featuring miracles wrought after his death, genealogies, and charters, but as mentioned earlier also features clumsy interpolations from the *Life of Illtyd.* Like that other 'warrior saint', Cadoc, whose baptised name *Cathmail* or *Cadfael* meant 'Battle Prince', also had associations with Arthur[104].

Cadoc was a grandson or possible great-grandson of Brychan, born to Gwladys and Gwynllyw, King of Gwynllywg and the story of his parents is told under Gwladys in Chapter 7[105]. He was educated at Caerwent by Tathan[106], and his *Life* tells how the pious boy brought burning hot coals to his master in his cloak and remained unharmed. On becoming a man, the 'Battle Prince' had no desire to

104 He is named in a later triad alongside Illtyd and Peredur as one of Arthur's 'three knights of upright judgement' and it has been conjectured he was the basis of Sir Galahad.

105 Some sources give Cadoc as a son of Brychan but this is probably a mistake for his son Rydoch.

106 Called by his pet name 'Meuthi' in the text.

take up the military role set out for him by his father and was taken in by his uncle Pawl of Penychen, in Glamorgan. Wandering Pawl's lands, Cadoc came face to face with a boar, and set up the boundaries of his monastery of Llancarfan according to the points where the boar turned to face him.

Having established his primary centre, Cadoc spent three years in Ireland after which he returned to the land of his grandfather Brychan accompanied by his pupils Finnian and Macmoil to learn Latin from an Italian named Bachan. Brychan granted Cadoc land at Llanspyddid which Cadoc left in the charge of Bachan before returning to Llancarfan to find his beloved foundation in ruins. He set about rebuilding with the aid of his pupils and the help of some stags which drew the wagons, giving rise to the monastery's alternative name of *Nant Carfan,* meaning Valley/Stream of the Stag.

Baring-Gould believes that before his return to Llancarfan, Cadoc established himself at Llangadog in Dyfed and that it was here the episode in which Cadoc was harassed by the ruler Sawyl Benuchel took place (1907 vol.2: 19). The men of this local chief broke into the monastery and stole food and drink. On discovering the theft, Cadoc ordered his monks to shave the heads of the men as they slept, and oddly in a callous pre-Christian style of revenge, to cut the lips and ears from their horses[107]. Further to this, on being confronted by Cadoc, it is told that the earth swallowed the men up for their thievery.

It was around this time that the book says the Synod of Brefi occurred, David being assured by an angel that the superior Cadoc would be abroad at the time. Cadoc is given as being on pilgrimage on Jerusalem, the most worthy of absences. On his return he learnt of the Synod taking place without him and of the exaltation of David, and so, furious at being overlooked, decided to 'fast against' David, until he was persuaded by an angel to stop and "forgave David his fault"[108].

Building from this, the Life gives account of Cadoc's victories over the secular powers of the time and establishes his rights and privileges. This begins with Cadoc sending King Arthur the gifts of a

107 This method of mutilation can also be found in the Celtic story of Branwen, told in the *Mabinogion.*

108 The practice of 'fasting against' someone involved starving oneself outside your enemy's walls, until they were shamed into giving in to your demands.

boar, beehive and hawk from a tree he found near Neath, by way of saying he intended to make a foundation there. That Cadoc was not enamoured by Arthur's kingly fame cannot be denied. A story follows in which Cadoc gives sanctuary to Ligessauc Long Hand, a man wanted for the deaths of three of Arthur's men. Cadoc sheltered the man for seven years and when Arthur found out, was held accountable for having kept the criminal in secret for so long. Arguing from opposing sides of the River Usk, Cadoc offered nine oxen as recompense for the dead men, but Arthur was childishly awkward about what colour he preferred. However, when the requested red and white cows were brought to the middle of the ford in the river and came into the hands of Arthur's men Cai and Bedivere, they turned into bundles of ferns! Humbled by the miracle, Arthur exchanged forgiveness with Cadoc and was said to have instated the law that Cadoc could extend sanctuary to a person for seven years, seven months and seven days.

As in the *Lives* of so many other saints, Maelgwyn Gwynedd also plays the role of aggressor in Cadoc's. The king's men arrived in Gwynllywg demanding tribute and abducting the daughter of Cadoc's steward. A fight ensued between them and the men of Gwynllwg and war looked to be unavoidable between the provinces until Cadoc appeared in a cloud of mist outside the tent of Maelgwyn, chastising him for his crimes and no doubt scaring him into submission. Following this, Maelgwyn promised Llancarfan would be safe from his forces and ensured his son Rhun swore the same. However Gwynllywg faced invasion not only from Gwynedd, but from the forces of his own uncle, Rhain, son of Brychan. Although Cadoc's father Gwynllyw's death occurs later in the text, it evidently occurred earlier than the invasion as the men were leaderless when they captured Rhain, and were scared to put to death the uncle of the heir of their country. Cadoc secured Rhain's release and obtained his promise to abide by the treaties already sworn by Arthur and Maelgwyn, showing the subjection of all three powers to Llancarfan.

The *Life* gives a story of Cadoc greatly desiring a bell which Gildas was delivering to Rome, which he later returned to Cadoc on account of the Pope recognising the saint's worthiness. An almost identical account is given in Illtyd's *Life* where Gildas is delivering a bell to Saint David who relinquishes it to the saint. Illtyd's author not only borrows this occurrence but transforms the tale of the men being swallowed by the earth into the occasion of Illtyd's conversion (see above).

Gildas' *Life* by Caradoc of Llancarfan tells us that Cadoc left Gildas in charge of Llancarfan for a year; most likely when he decided to travel to the North[109]. Whilst digging the foundations for a new monastery Cadoc discovered the bones of a giant man and in prayer discovered they belonged to Caw, who had ruled in Strathclyde. Presumably it is intended that this was Gildas' father, and Cadoc raised his monastery over his grave in respect. On Cadoc's return to take up his position at Llancarfan, Gildas moved on to Glastonbury but the two friends stayed in contact, spending Lent every year near each other on the isles in the Bristol Channel, Gildas going to Steep Holm and Cadoc to Flat Holm. The *Life* says that the rocks around Flat Holm were called 'The Wolves' because two wolves had swum there to kill and devour Cadoc's sheep and were, rather unfairly, turned to stone for following their nature.

Cadoc also visited Brittany and went via Cornwall, where he met his aunt Saint Keyne (see Chapter 1) and also elicited a spring at Harlyn Bay, near Padstow. It is said he returned with water from the Holy Land, gathered from the River Jordan, which he poured into the well, strengthening its already miraculous healing qualities.

It is clear that Llancarfan had grown in size and wealth, Cadoc having inherited Gwynllyw's lands and those of his Uncle Paul of Penychen. Towards the end of his life, the upkeep of such a large monastery was too much for Cadoc, and was thus entrusted to his disciple Elli. Cadoc departed, carried 'in a cloud' (most probably meaning by boat) to the monastery of Beneventum, which had lost its abbot, and was appointed their replacement until the time came for Cadoc also to leave this world. Scholarly opinion tends to regard the destination of Beneventum in Southern Italy to be highly improbable, and suggest instead he went to Bannaventa, now Weedon in Northamptonshire, where he was most likely martyred by the Saxons in old age[110].

A friend of Cadoc and the other great holy man of South Wales of the time, who has been mentioned in several of the *Lives* of other saints, is **Dyfrig**, or Dubricius, to give him his Latin appellation.

---

109 Although Caradoc revised Cadoc's *Life* besides writing that of Gildas', there is a discrepancy where he says Cadoc was in Scotland for seven years.
110 This confusing and most probably inaccurate move to Southern Italy possibly arose from the notion that Cadoc was called 'the wise' and Beneventum was dedicated to St Sophia, whose name also means wisdom. It is therefore pretended that he came there and was called Sophias by the inhabitants. Yet the epithet 'Doeth' (the Wise) was not used until about the seventeenth century (Baring-Gould and Fisher 1907 vol.2: 40).

Dyfrig is often thought of as founder of Llandaff, partly through mistake and partly through design of the twelfth-century compilers of its history. Dyfrig's lands and churches lay mostly along the English border, an area decimated by Saxon raids in the sixth century. After the Battle of Deorham, Llandaff received some of Dyfrig's disciples fleeing from Ergyng, taking them in and also obtaining their gospels. During the compilation of the *Book of Llandaff,* notes made in the margin of a Book of Gospels about grants made to Dyfrig were fleshed out by the compilers, using their own knowledge of the areas and boundaries and also The Church of Llandaff's own motives for laying claim to lands granted to Dyfrig[111]. These deserted sites had been reoccupied by monks of Llandaff in the centuries following the raids and proof of an unbroken line of inheritance from Dyfrig was desirable to them.

Dyfrig's *Life* begins with a miracle. His grandfather, Peibio, King of Ergyng, on discovering his daughter was pregnant, angrily had her tied up in a bag and thrown in the river to drown[112]. She survived this, and consequently being burnt alive, being found the next morning nursing the newborn Dyfrig amongst the ashes. The king was a sufferer of a leprous affliction that caused him to continuously dribble, but when the baby was brought before him and touched his cheek, Peibio was miraculously cured. His attitude was there changed and he granted his grandson land on the spot where he was born, which is Madley in Herefordshire[113].

We do not know much about Dyfrig's early life, where he was schooled or who consecrated him bishop. Early in his adult life he

---

111 The grants of land mentioned include Cilhal (possibly Pencoyd, Herefordshire), granted by King Erb. This is puzzling as Erb was father of Peibio and therefore supposedly Dyfrig's great grandfather, and Dyfrig would not have been young when he received them as the names of witnesses given were pupils of his. It seems unlikely that the adult Dyfrig's great-grandfather was alive to sign these lands to him himself, which throws doubt upon his family tree (Baring-Gould and Fisher 1907 vol.2: 364)

112 Similarly to David's nickname 'The Waterman', Dyfrig's name seems to derive from *Dyfrwr,* or 'Waterling', referring perhaps to the miracle of his birth. The *Life* of Teilo mentions seven sons, who Teilo saved from being drowned by a poor man who could not afford to feed them. Teilo raised them and they became known as the Dyfrwyr as they were found in water and ate only fish. They were later sent to Dyfrig. This is another trope of the times; a variation appears in one version of Samson's *Life,* by Bishop Alanus of Auxerre, that Samson was one of seven brothers born to one mother who sent them to be drowned but were saved and grew up to be the seven saints of Brittany.

113 Peibio is sometimes stated as Dyfrig's father, as is Brychan, but is likely these were both his grandfathers, as one of the sons of Brychan was called Pabiali, possibly giving rise to the confusion.

founded Hentland, near his birthplace. He went from there to found another monastery and decided to site it where he found a white sow and her piglets, calling it Mochros, 'Swine Moor' (now Moccas)[114]. These were large sites, either of which could have been Dyfrig's 'arch-monastery', which perhaps led to the misunderstanding around the saint's status as an 'archbishop'. Archbishop at this time meant only that the abbot ruled over his subordinate monasteries, not over other bishops. This term was misunderstood in later years and taken to mean the latter.

The *Book of Llandaff* records Teilo and Samson as his pupils but the former was under Paulinus and the latter under Illtyd, although consecrated priest and bishop by Dyfrig. A long list of his other disciples follows, who it says Dyfrig sent out into the country to found new churches, and that he had been made Archbishop by Germanus, and was able to ordain bishops from his seat at Llandaff. This history was of course all retroactively inserted to suit the church's contemporary needs, and this list of disciples matched the list of churches that Llandaff wished to claim. The majority of these lands of Dyfrig are in Ergyng where he was born but he also had a church in Penally, on the coast of Pembrokeshire near Caldey Island where he would spend Lent, and where he placed Samson as Abbot following Piro's ungainly drunken fall. Dyfrig also had influence at, but not authority over, Llantwit, as shown in the *Life of Illtyd*.

The last great event in the life of Saint Dyfrig was the council of Llanddewi Brefi, which Dyfrig called in support of Germanus of Auxerre's war on the Pelagian Heresy. It is supposed that he died shortly after this, c.546. In 1120, Dyfrig's remains were moved from their resting place in Bardsey to Llandaff where he was named its patron alongside Peter, Teilo, and Euddogwy. It is doubtful that he had anything to do with the founding of Llandaff. Its influence only began to grow under the successor of Teilo, Euddogwy, and his successor Berthguin, when the abandoned sites of Dyfrig began to be repopulated in the seventh century. The aim of Bishop Urban in the twelfth century under whom the *Book of Llandaff* was written was to prove rightful ownership of these lands by stating that Dyfrig had ruled as Archbishop of Llandaff.

Geoffrey of Monmouth further complicated things by his

---

114 This method of situating a monastery by the finding of a sow and her young is a theme well used in other saints' *Lives* including Cadog, Brynach, Paul Aurelian, and Kentigern.

fabrication that Aurelius Ambrosius named Dyfrig Archbishop of Caerleon and Samson Archbishop of York in 429. He has Dyfrig crown King Arthur and then retire, passing on his episcopal see to David. This story was repeated by Benedict of Gloucester and also Gerald of Wales, whose assurance that the pall had passed from Caerleon to Menevia (St. Davids) suited his own claims to the independence of St. Davids from Canterbury as a Metropolitan see. In actuality, Dyfrig had as much to do in life with Caerleon as he did with Llandaff and the entire story was a fiction, but shows the importance and respect his name carried with it.

The motives of Urban and the Church of Llandaff in the twelfth century are clear and the *Lives* of the saints in the *Book of Llandaff* tell us a lot more about the period they were written than the actual days of these holy men. It is clear that the brief mention of Teilo being schooled under Dyfrig before being sent to Paulinus is an insertion in an attempt to bring the Teilo churches in the see of St. David's under the arm of Llandaff as well as its designs on those belonging to Hereford. If we remove this political gloss and the unhelpful throwing around of terms like 'archbishop' we can glimpse the simple lives of these men who lived mostly in harmony, occasionally in contention, but ultimately for the good of extending their faith, not their own political boundaries.

Chapter 7

A Miscellany of Saints

Below are listed, in glossary form, some of the notable saints of Wales, Somerset, Devon, and Cornwall who perhaps did not fit the themes of the other chapters yet warrant a place within this book.

Beuno

Beuno was a highly peripatetic saint who left foundations in many places across North Wales. Born of the royal house of Powys to parents Bugi and Beren in their old age, Beuno was sent to Caerwent, Chepstow, for his education. He rose to the rank of priest, and the monastery's founder, Ynyr, the ruler of Gwent, even became his disciple in his old age and gave him land at Llanveynoe, now in Herefordshire. Beuno then returned to his birthplace of Berriew in Powys to give his father his last rites, and by his grave he planted an acorn from which a mighty oak grew. This tree had a branch which curved down into the earth and back out again, and one local saying was that if an Englishman passed under the branch he would drop dead but if a Welshman did, he would be unharmed. All trees on ground dedicated to Beuno were deemed sacred.

Another nationalistic tradition recorded in Beuno's *Life* relates that he was walking near the Severn when he heard the voices of Saxon huntsmen from across the water. Beuno returned to his disciples and urged them to stay away from the lands of these foreigners who he foresaw overrunning Wales. He left his foundation at Berriew to a disciple and continued further into North Wales, receiving land from a king named Cynan at Gwyddelwern. Here he ran into trouble with relations of Cynan who demanded food and board from Beuno, the story running almost identically to that of Brynach's altercation with Maelgwn Gwynedd (see below). The young lords slaughtered an ox belonging to Beuno, the meat of which then stubbornly refused to cook. This encounter did not end so happily, with Beuno cursing the men and moving back to Powys. Here he had family, and instructed his niece Gwenfrewi (Winifred) who became a highly venerated saint in Wales and has her own entry below[115].

Beuno exchanged a gold sceptre he had been given by Cynan for land from Cadwallon, King of Gwynedd, but soon found out this land had been wrongly reappropriated. Beuno angrily demanded different lands from Cadwallon or that he return the gift of the sceptre, but the king refused and said he had already given the sceptre away. The restless saint departed Cadwallon's lands, cursing the king, but before long came to the domain of the king's cousin Gwyddaint who granted him land at Clynnog ('the place of holly trees') without tribute, where Beuno happily settled and created his greatest monastic foundation.

A carpenter from another of Beuno's settlements, Aberffraw in Anglesey, was working on a palace in Caerwent when the king Ynyr's daughter Tegiwg fell in love with him, and was sent home with him to be his wife. Their feelings for one another may have not been exactly mutual, as the carpenter abandoned (or some say possibly even murdered) her on the way. She was found by shepherds of Beuno who took her to Clynnog where the saint revived her and took her into his monastic community. Tegiwg's brother Iddon, having heard of her misadventures, pursued them to retrieve his sister, but Tegiwg preferred to stay and follow a religious life rather than return in embarrassment to Caerwent. Iddon accepted this but demanded the return of the gold and horses which the carpenter had taken along with his sister. Beuno mediated between the carpenter, Iddon, and King Cadwallon, and reportedly had to restore the carpenter's head to his shoulders and revive him after Iddon struck it from him in a rage.

After this eventful life Beuno remained the rest of his days in Clynnog, where he died and was buried. Like Teilo, a story survives of his body miraculously multiplying into three to satisfy the claims of Clynnog, Nevin, and Bardsey to house his corpse. His well,

---

115 Darrell Wolcott believes the Beuno who was son of Bugi and uncle of Winifred to be a separate earlier saint of Holywell dating to the mid fifth century, and that the Beuno whose foundation was at Clynnog, and to whom the rest of the legends relate, was actually a son of Cynan. The contemporaries mentioned in his *Life* date him to the mid sixth century and Wolcott believes his deeds were amalgamated with the earlier Beuno in the writing of his *Life* which was appended to that of Winifred. (Wolcott, D. ancientwelshstudies.org).

Ffynnon Feuno, was said to cure children of epilepsy and rickets if they were dipped in it and then spent the night on a bed of rushes on top of Beuno's tombstone. In the seventeenth century it was believed that a sick person sleeping on Beuno's tomb on a Friday would recover – or die within three weeks! (Breverton 2000: 78).

Another tradition states that Beuno blessed the curlew after losing his prayer book whilst crossing the sands of the Menai Strait. On returning to his cell, he found the book with a curlew sitting beside it. In gratitude, he prayed for the protection of the species and this is said to be why the eggs of the bird are camouflaged and so difficult to find.

Brynach

Saint Brynach is thought to have been the priest and close friend of the similarly-named patriarch Brychan. Iolo Morgannwg believed Brynach travelled with Brychan from Ireland when he came to make his foundation at Brecon, and married one of his friend's many daughters, Cymorth. His children by Cymorth include a son Berwyn and three daughters, Gwenan, Mwynen, and Gwenlliw. His *Life* does not mention these figures but rather said that after performing miracles in Rome and Brittany he came to Wales, landing at Milford Haven. Here he was targeted by the 'daughter of a nobleman' acting as a vessel for the Devil, whose attempts at seduction failed and turned into attempts at murder[116].

Brynach was active in Carmarthenshire and Pembrokeshire but was unable to settle until reaching Nevern, near Newport (Pembs.). This land was granted by Clechre (Clether), his wife's brother. Impressed by Brynach's piety, Clechre yielded his lands to him as well as entrusting him with the education of his sons before departing to Cornwall (see Chapter 1). At this time Brynach also had an encounter with the notorious king Maelgwn Gwynedd, who when travelling through Brynach's lands sent word ahead for the saint to receive him at his monastery and demanded he provide a meal for his entourage. The saint, refusing to bow to pressure from a secular authority, declined, causing Maelgwn to fly into a rage. Brynach was in possession of a certain cow that gave abundant milk which Maelgwn stole to feed his men, but try as they might, no

116 Whether this was Cymorth may be conjectured; Baring-Gould suggests the story was altered to remove the details of it having been Brynach's wife that tried to have him killed (or the fact that he had a family at all) so as not to offend twelfth century sensibilities (1907 vol.2: 219).

amount of heat applied would cook the meat, which stayed stubbornly cold. Perceiving the miracle, Maelgwn and his men went humbly to Brynach and confessed their crime. Brynach graciously forgave them and in typical Saints' *Lives* style, restored the cow to life. He also miraculously provided a feast for the men, and in thanks Maelgwn bestowed the land of the monk Thelych upon him.

Traditions exist that Saint David was a friend of Brynach's and would call by to see him on his way to Llanddewi Brefi. On one occasion David was carrying a huge carved standing stone which was procured from him by Brynach and was said thereafter to stand in Nevern churchyard, perhaps the origin story of the Vitalianus stone which dates from approximately 500 CE. The remarkably well preserved and tall 'Nevern cross' stands nearby and dates from the late tenth or early eleventh century. At the entrance to the picturesque churchyard is the famous 'bleeding yew', the red sap of which has been linked into the mysteries and folklore of the site. Besides foundations in Wales, Brynach is associated with Braunton in Devon where he is known as Saint Brannoc. He was said to have sailed there in a stone sarcophagus and founded a church where he came across a white sow with her brood.

Buriana

The name of the parish of St. Buryan near Land's End is variously thought to mean a burial ground, or derive from the name Buriana or Berriona which translates to 'Irish Lady'. Buriana was identified by Leland with Bruinech, who was a kinswoman of the Irish saint Ciaran of Saighir (Saint Piran), and may have accompanied him to Cornwall. Local legend tells how she was carried off by a certain lord Geraint in the midst of winter who would not return her to Piran until he heard a cuckoo call at dawn. This story is derived from Ciaran's *Life* in which Bruniech was a virgin in his mother's convent of Cill Liadain and her abductor was a man of Meath called Dima. Ciaran fasted outside Dima's castle walls until he released Bruinech. In this version rather than a cuckoo it was a swan, stork, or heron that was heard. However, Dima tried once again to abduct Bruinech whom he had claimed as his wife but on reaching Cill Liadain found her dead. Dima blamed Ciaran and raged at the saint, but was rendered powerless by him, and shortly afterwards discovered that his dun had caught fire by God's vengeance. Ciaran resurrected Bruinech, having earlier also miraculously removed her pregnancy, leaving her free to continue her religious calling and follow him to Cornwall.

Leland records that in 930 the Saxon King Æthelstan had a church built on the site of Buriana's oratory after passing through and praying there for success in his coming battle on the Scilly Isles with the Danes, which he won. The church was of some importance and had the parishes of Sennen and St. Levan under it as daughter houses. The charter of Æthelstan meant that St. Buryan answered to the monarchy rather than the Bishops of Exeter which led to much ill will. The parish was notably excommunicated in 1238 for eight years after a violent fight in the churchyard between the monarch's Dean, the Bishop's Prebend and 41 others. The church's own guidebook labels St Buryan "The wickedest parish in Cornwall"!

Govan

This saint's chapel is one of the most unusual and picturesque in Wales. The tiny thirteenth century building stands on the site of the hermit's cell built into the rocks below the cliffs on the most southerly tip of the Pembrokeshire coast, a true spot of isolation. Behind the chapel is a cleft of rock into which Saint Govan supposedly squeezed to escape from pirates, and markings on it are said to be the impressions of his ribs where the rock miraculously closed around him in protection. Govan vowed to protect the coast from further marauders by ringing a bell whenever any approached. This obviously made him unpopular with the pirates who made off with his bell, but it was miraculously returned and enshrined within Bell Rock for safe keeping, which allegedly made a loud metallic sound when struck thereafter. Steps lead down from the chapel to a holy well with a multitude of healing properties attributed to it, although sadly now run dry. Govan's body is said to be buried beneath the altar in the chapel and the steps down to the chapel itself are said to be enchanted and impossible to number without losing count.

Not much is known about this hermit although some claim Govan may be the Arthurian knight Gawain, who retired here to live out his days and serve God. This is most likely due to Gawain's name being rendered *Gauvain* in French (although Gwalchmai in Welsh). His name appears to be linked to the Irish smith deity, Govannon, mentioned in *Culhwch and Olwen* although in the story he appears as a separate entity to Gwalchmai. William of Malmesbury believed Gawain to be buried further inland from St. Govan's Chapel at Castell Gwalchmai in Rhos, Pembrokeshire. It is suggested that Gawain is buried at another Ross, (on Wye), and this is perhaps why we find another church of St Govan relatively nearby in Llangovan, Monmouthshire. Baring-Gould does not consider the Govan of West Wales to be associated with that church but rather that the saint's origin is the Irish Gobhan, disciple of Ailbe and Abbot of Dairinis (1907 vol.3: 143).

Gwladys and Gwynllyw

Eldest of the many daughters of Brychan, Gwladys is notable for becoming the wife of the warlord Gwynllyw, or rather being abducted as such. Gwynllyw was ruler of Gwynllwg, a kingdom in modern day South Glamorgan now identified as Wentloog, who was later converted by his son, Cadoc, and was notably also the brother (or possibly uncle) of Saint Petroc. Gwynllyw's own *Life* of course paints him in a favourable light: enamoured by the beauty of Gwladys, he sought permission from Brychan for his daughter's hand in marriage. However, in their son Cadoc's *Life,* which is thought to be the earlier of the two and the more accurate, we are told that Gwynllyw took Gwladys by force. In this version Brychan angrily turned away Gwynllyw's proposal so the southern king gathered three hundred men and marched on Talgarth, the royal seat of Brycheiniog and abducted the maiden. Brychan's men pursued and slew two-thirds of the party, but on reaching the border of his own country, Gwynllyw happened upon King Arthur, accompanied by his men Cai and Bedivere. Despite Arthur's own desire for the young woman with Gwynllyw, and the temptation to take her for himself, he reasoned after listening to his companions that Gwynllyw was within his rights so assisted in ridding him of his enemy. The appearance here of Arthur as adjudicator is pure fable, especially as he, Cai, and Bedivere appear again for an altercation with the adult Cadoc later in the *Life*!

Gwynllyw 'lawfully' married his captive bride who bore him a son. Four shining orbs hung in the air in the corners of Gwladys' room from the night of conception to the night of Cadoc's birth. Cadoc's *Life* tells us that following this, Gwynllyw continued in his bold and ruthless ways until Cadoc, with Gwladys' help, convinced his father to renounce his sinful ways and both parents were converted by his hand.

Both Gwladys and Gwynllyw retired as hermits, Gwladys supposedly settling on the bank of the River Ebbw at Bassaleg, Newport, where her grave is said to be. She is also associated with Capel Wladus in Gelligaer. The church built on the site of Gwynllyw's cell at Stow Hill became the foundation for, and was incorporated into, Newport Cathedral, dedicated to Saint Woolos – a corruption of his name.

Perhaps mirroring his violent and warlike life, posthumous miracles attested to at Gwynllyw's shrine relate to war and plunder. The *Life of Gwynllyw* tells us Viking pirates pillaged the church at Stow Hill and retreated in their ships but they were assailed by a terrible vision of the figure of Gwynllyw, riding them down on all sides and buffeting their ships with heavy winds which drove them into each other and wrecked their remains on rocks. The church was further plundered by Saxon raiders but the cheeses that were amongst their spoils ran with blood when cut into. The *Life* suggests that despite the Saxon king Harold making a hasty confession after this omen, the violation was the reason for his defeat and death in battle at Hastings.

Helen/Elen

Saint Helen is a popular figure in Britain, yet a confusing one to unravel, due to the confounding of several personages. Helena of Constantinople, mother of the fourth century Emperor Constantine and discoverer of the True Cross, became associated with Britain in the Early Middle Ages when a tradition that she was the daughter of the British king Coel was propagated by Geoffrey of Monmouth. Historical evidence suggests she was a native of Asia Minor, yet the association with Britain endured and she became the patron of, amongst other places, Coel's seat of Colchester.

Association of this Helen with Britain may have been further compounded by confusion with Saint Elen of Caernarfon, especially as both Helens had a son named Constantine, or Cystennin in the case of the Welsh Helen. This native princess was married to Magnus Maximus, when he took command of the Roman base of Segontium at Caernarfon and its troops. Maximus was a Spanish officer who had risen to become Emperor of Britain, and placed himself in opposition to the Roman Emperor Gratian. He took troops to Gaul and managed to oust Gratian from Gaul and Spain and continued on towards Rome. Elen and her brothers accompanied Maximus to Gaul and the Welsh Triads say that her epithet Elen Luyddog – 'Elen of the Hosts' came from her marching at the head of one of the legions or 'hosts' (Barber and Pickett 1997: 18). Whilst in Gaul, it is said Elen and Macsen met the influential Saint Martin of Tours who inspired Elen, and when Maximus pressed on to Italy, she returned to Britain and spread the Christian message.

This history is romanticised in the Welsh story recorded in the *Mabinogion* in *The Dream of Macsen Wledig*, in which a vision of Elen is seen by Macsen Wledig, which is the Welsh rendering of Magnus Maximus. Falling in love and desiring to make Elen his Empress, Macsen sent scouts to find her, which they did, although rather than agreeing to go with them, Elen requested the Emperor come to her. He was eventually led to her home in Caernarfon, where everything was as it had been in his dream, including Elen's two brothers Cynan and Adeon playing chess nearby and her father Eudaf carving chess pieces. Elen agreed to be his wife and as a gift she asked for the island of Britain for her father and for three castles to be constructed at Caernarfon, Carmarthen, and Caerleon. She also requested roads be built to connect all the castles, and the story says it was this innovation that earned her the title of 'Elen of the Hosts'. Traces of the Roman roads remain today including sections of the road to Carmarthen and although their existence predates Elen's time, they are known as Sarn Helen or Ffordd Elen, meaning Elen's Causeway or Road. Macsen stayed in Britain for seven years, and in this time the Romans elected a new Emperor, but with the aid of Elen's brothers, Macsen and his army retook Rome.

Elen is proposed by some to represent the sovereignty goddess of Britain and in wedding her, Macsen weds the land and receives from her the divine right to rule. Taking this further, to some neo-pagans she is the antlered goddess Elen of the Ways, patron of roads and travellers, a shadowy figure who is said to be associated with deer and the migratory trackways of these animals and of the ancient people of the land. Archaeological evidence of her cult is scarce, leading many to doubt its original existence at all.

There are several wells dedicated to Helen throughout Wales but few churches, which include Caernarfon and Llanelan in Monmouthshire and a now extinct one in Gower, however in all of these cases, we cannot be entirely sure whether the initial dedication was to Elen Luyddog or Helen of Constantinople. Similarly, the Cornish dedications to Helen could be to either of these saints, or Helen the companion of Breaca, or another still. Besides Cystennin (Gorneu, who was commemorated at Llangystennin, see Chapter 5), Elen and Maximus were reported to

Above: St. Helen of Caernarvon: This painting depicts the mysterious nature of this saintly queen, the chess piece representing her sovereignty and the deer linking her to legends of Elen and her trackways. Acrylic on canvas (20in x 24 in).

have had four other sons, Peblig, Owain Finddu, Ednyfed, and Gwythyr; and many of the royal houses of Britain claim lineage from them, having the twofold strength of Elen's royal British descent coupled with the blood of a Roman Emperor.

Melangell

One of the saintly descendants of Elen and Macsen Wledig, Melangell was a sixth century abbess and patron saint of hares, her name meaning 'Sweet Angel'. Besides Winifred, she is the only female Welsh saint to receive her own Latin *Life,* in which she is known as 'Monacella'. This fifteenth century *Life* gives her Irish origins and tells of her escape from a marriage arranged by her father, King Iowchel. Fleeing to Wales, she settled in the valley of Pennant, on the Powys/Gwynedd border and lived in solitude for fifteen years. Then, in the year 604, her peace was disturbed by the hunting party of a certain Prince Brochwel Ysgythrog[117] who was in pursuit of a hare with his hounds. The hare evaded Brochwel, disappeared into a thicket where Melangell was seated reading her prayers, and promptly hid under her gown. On reaching the clearing, Brochwel was at once struck by the radiance of the holy Melangell; but his dogs recoiled from the prey they had been chasing moments before, and fled.

Impressed by the piety of the young woman, Brochwel granted the land on which he had been hunting to Melangell, and henceforth Pennant Melangell became a sanctuary for all animals. Tradition tells that it was especially unlucky to kill hares there, which were regarded as 'Melangell's little lambs' (Breverton 2000: 400-1). Here she established a convent of virgins and a place for those seeking sanctuary. The privileges awarded by Brochwel endured and continued to be honoured by the following generations, and an echo of them can even be found today in the Saint Melangell Centre, a place for retreat, quiet contemplation and counselling.

Right: St. Melangell: The Welsh patroness of animals and nature, Melangell shelters the hare in the folds of her gown from the hounds of the local prince who cannot pass beyond the tangle of blackberry thorns surrounding her holy glade. Acrylic on wood (12in x 18in).

---

117 Who later became father to Saint Tesilio.

The church itself is also of particular interest. Although the legend of Melangell is relatively late, evidence of the importance of her cult exists from centuries before. Despite the relics of Melangell being lost in the Reformation, bones thought to belong to the saint were discovered in 1958 and her shrine was pieced back together

from the fragments of stone that had been used elsewhere in the church and its churchyard walls. Although the church itself is cautious about stating the authenticity of the bones, author Nick Mayhew Smith suggests the likelihood of them being genuine, hidden away by fervent followers of the saint who refused to destroy both a fourteenth century stone effigy of Melangell and a fifteenth century rood screen depicting her tale (2011: 455). These remarkable survivals, combined with the impressive and rare shrine, add to the site's overwhelming sense of holiness, which is amplified by the beautiful natural surroundings which Melangell treasured so much.

Neot

Despite being born in the ninth century in Anglo-Saxon territory, Neot became an important and beloved saint in Cornwall, and the stories of his miracles heavily mirror the legends of the other Celtic saints. Various versions of his *Life* exist from the eleventh century onwards, although the existence of an early Anglo-Saxon *Life* written shortly after Neot's death is mentioned in the work of Asser, a contemporary of King Alfred, but it was sadly lost.

The alternate *Lives* give differing names for his father including Fidulf, Eldulf, Edulph and Adulph, which may all be regarded as variations of King Æthelwulf of Wessex who was father of the Saxon kings Æthelbald, Æthelbert, Æthelred, and Alfred. Rev. Baring-Gould conjectures that Neot was an illegitimate son (1907, vol.4: 6) and Whitaker takes this even further, suggesting he may be one and the same with Æthelstan, Æthelwulf's eldest illegitimate progeny, who strangely disappears from history after his victory over the Danes at Sandwich (1809: 72-4). It could be conjectured that his story was then taken up in that of Neot, who entered the monastery at Glastonbury and perhaps thus changed his name on retiring from the military world[118].

118 Other scholars are more wary about proclaiming Neot's prestigious birth, some preferring to assert he was the youngest offspring of Æthelwulf, others erring even more on the side of caution and theorising that he was a

After a time spent as sacristan at Glastonbury Abbey, Neot travelled to Cornwall to the southern reaches of Bodmin Moor, where he may have given his name to Menheniot - 'Sanctuary of Neot' - before moving on to Hamstoke, the Saxon name for what later became St. Neot. Here he raised an oratory with a fish pond and Celtic cross where he dwelt for seven years before making a pilgrimage to Rome seeking an audience with the Pope. The details of his life and journey are depicted in the stained glass of the church of St. Neot to this day.

On Neot's return he established a college but did not have many people to preach to. Tradition holds that the local farmers would not leave their fields unguarded from the hordes of crows which assaulted their crops in order to come to listen to him preach. The story goes that Neot led the crows to an old Roman camp nearby where he bade them remain until he finished preaching.

Other miracles related about the saint include familiar Celtic tropes. Like Petroc, Neot sheltered a fleeing deer, and on discovering the saint, the huntsman renounced his worldly ways and entered a monastery. The common motif of deer pulling his ploughs after his oxen were stolen is also featured.

More specific stories relate to Neot's small stature, which is claimed to be as little as four feet thus earning him the title of the Pygmy Saint! Glastonbury Abbey supposedly had an iron stool he used to preach from and to reach the church door lock, but on one occasion when he did not have the stool with him, the lock miraculously descended so he could reach it. Perhaps the fact behind the legend may have been that they had the height of the lock altered for his ease? Similarly, at the church of St. Neot, he had a stone from which he would throw the key into the lock, the key always finding its mark.

Perhaps the most famous story associated with Neot tells of his fabled fish pond which would always contain two fish despite Neot taking one a day for his sustenance. One day when Neot fell ill, an over-zealous servant cooked up both fish, which sorely troubled the saint rather than pleased him as was intended. He ordered the boiled and fried fish to be returned to the water which at once restored them to life. With order being resumed, so was Neot's good

---

more distant relation of Alfred from the royal houses of the Saxons whose connection was exaggerated by his later biographers (Gorman 1820: 22-6).

health[119].

Asser's *Life of Alfred* tells how the king visited his elder brother and received harsh advice from the saint who berated Alfred for not listening to his petitioners. Neot also appeared to Alfred after his death assuring him of victory in the Battle of Edington which occurred in the year 878.

Saint Neot's body remained in the Cornish church until 974 when an earl of Huntingdonshire desired the bones of a saint to attract pilgrims to his new priory and bribed the Cornish priest in possession of them to abscond with them. Despite the attempts of angry Cornishmen to reclaim them, the relics remained in their new location which became known as the town of St. Neots, Cambridgeshire.

Paul Aurelian

The ninth century *Life* of Saint Paul, who is variously known as Paul Aurelian and Pol de Léon, was written by a cleric of Landévennec called Wrmonoc who allegedly worked from an older source. The *Life* tells that Paul was born into a large family in Penychen, South Glamorgan. At a young age he joined the monastery of St. Illtyd at Llantwit Major, and was for some time on Caldey Island, against the wishes of his father. Amongst his companions here were David, Gildas, and Samson, and Chapter 6 covers some of the varying accounts of the same events in their lives in which one saint or the other is elevated to give them the most prominent role.

When a little older, Paul settled on his father's land, building an oratory where he withdrew from the world for some time. After a while he tired of this and visited the court of King Marc (see Chapter 5), although the strong-willed saint and king clashed, and Paul left his lands, refusing the request that he stay there as Marc's bishop. He continued on to the settlement of his sister in Cornwall where he helped her to raise a sea wall and this story is sometimes given as proof that Paul was the founder of the church and parish of his name near Penzance[120].

---

119 This is one of the stories depicted in the well preserved stained glass of the church of St. Neot.

120 Baring-Gould regards this sister as Wulvella, stating her as the founder of Gulval parish. However the only named sister in the *Life* is Sicofolia who Baring-Gould takes to be Exeter saint Sativola/Sidwell, the details of whose

There is of course difficulty in identifying sites that were dedicated to Paul Aurelian rather than to Paul the Apostle. The association of the village of Paul with Paul Aurelian has been questioned by historians as has the association of other south-westerly sites such as Staverton in Devon. The latter of these places, according to Orme, was only associated with Paul Aurelian in the 1920s by speculation and a bout of Celtic revivalism (1996: 203).

Besides the confusion with the obvious famous apostle of the same name, many writers have struggled to reconcile the various other Pauls, and Paul Aurelian is frequently confounded with Paulinus, the aged and blind tutor of St David, and also Pawl of Penychen, the noble on whose land St Illtyd was converted (see Chapter 6). Wrmonoc appears to draw on elements of both of these in his description of Paul Aurelian.

The *Life* states that Paul departed from the South-west of Britain for Armorica (Brittany), landing on the small island of Ushant (*Ouessant* in French) where he made his first Breton foundation. Moving on to the mainland, he landed at Lampaul Plouarzel and established himself at Ploudalmezeau, and his disciples radiated from here. Paul sought permission to settle in Léon from the local Count who coincidentally (or perhaps not) was a cousin of his from Wales called Withur. Gaining this and various gifts, he made a foundation in Ocsimor. Withur desired Paul be made bishop but, as with Marc, he resisted and had to have his hand forced by the king, Childebert.

Around the year 553, during the revolution instigated by Saint Samson against Conomor, the lord of Léon and Domnonia (see Chapter 6), Paul withdrew himself as head of his monastery, stating old age and ill health as his reason. The real cause may be more likely that he would be in a dangerous position politically, should he choose to support the revolt against the regent of his lands and it failed. His two successors as Abbot, Joevin and Tigernomagle, only lasted a year each but by this time the revolution had been a success and it was safe for Paul to return to his post, which he duly did. Although Conomor is not mentioned by name in Wrmonoc's *Life*, Baring-Gould theorises that he is signified by the dragon that

---

Life are inconsistent with Paul's. Canon Doble is far more cautious about associating either Sidwell or Wulvela with Paul however does assert his belief that the Cornish parish does belong to him rather than Paul the Apostle (1971: 158-60).

Paul rids the land of in his account (1907 vol.4: 83-4). After a rather lengthy return from retirement, Paul is said to have died at his monastery on the island of Batz in 579, aged around 100.

Rumon

Rumon is another seemingly prolific sixth-century saint that we know little about, and who is known under various appellations. He is known as Rumon or Ruan in Cornwall, where he has churches at Ruan Lanihorne, Ruan Minor, and Ruan Major. In Devon he is honoured at Tavistock Abbey and Romansleigh, which was under its rule. In Brittany he is known as Saint Renan or Ronan, and is regarded as the founder of Saint-Renan and Locronan.

He is given Irish origins in his *Life*, which states he came to Brittany and began attempting to convert the pagans of Cornouaille. He met with opposition from the wife of a peasant who he had befriended. She came to the court of the local king Grallo to accuse Ronan of being a werewolf who ravaged the peasant's sheep and had carried off and killed her daughter, who she had in fact hidden in a chest. Grallo promised to bring Ronan before his dogs who would surely attack and kill the man if there was any scent of wolf about him. The dogs, of course, greeted Ronan in friendly manner and all charges were dropped, and the girl was found on searching of the woman's house. The malicious woman did not abate from her persecution of Ronan and he relocated to Hillion in Domnonia where he spent the last of his days. His body was returned to Locronan after his death, where his tomb represents him as a bishop.

In 960, Tavistock Abbey in Devon translated his relics from Ruan Lanihorne, but how did they reach Cornwall and where do his Cornish dedications come from? The Breton *Life* makes no mention of him being in Cornwall, although logically he would have passed through on the passage from Ireland. Baring-Gould identifies him with Moruan, a disciple of Senan and one of the Irish band who populated south-west Cornwall (see Chapter 2). It was a common linguistic practice amongst Irish saints to add the prefix *mo-* to a name as a diminutive (1907 vol.4: 120). We may guess that Rumon established his Cornish foundations before moving on to Brittany, but this does not explain how his relics were claimed to lie in Ruan Lanihorne or Tavistock. Assuming they were not false, the only explanation may be that monks from Brittany fled the country with them when the Northmen began raiding their abbeys in the tenth century. William of Malmesbury, visiting Tavistock in 1120, saw the grave but no works on the *Life of Rumon*. The monks corrected this lack by adapting the Breton *Life* and unsurprisingly adding the last two resting places of Rumon's bones. By the thirteenth century, Glastonbury Abbey claimed the remains of Rumon, and purported him to be the brother of Saint Tudwal. Despite details on his life being scarce, Rumon must have been regarded in high esteem as a saint for him to have so many posthumous moves.

Senan

Saint Senan's name is said to mean "little wise old man" in Gaelic, an odd choice of name for a babe by its mother perhaps, but Senan's birth had been foretold by Saint Patrick, so his *Life* says, as the coming of a great teacher. When the birth came, his mother grasped a Rowan tree branch for support, which miraculously sprang into fruit. The omen of the Rowan, a tree that thrives in sparse habitats, was perhaps one which foretold Senan's harsh monastic lifestyle (Baring-Gould & Fisher 1907 vol.4: 184).

Senan was born to Geirrcinn/Ercan and Comgella in County Clare, Ireland. Proving in early life to be not cut out for a military career, Senan was sent by his parents to the monastery of Cassidus and later moved on to that of Saint Natalis at Kilnamanagh. A devout and bright boy, Senan soon outgrew the teachings of his master and was sent to found his own monastery. He eventually did this at Inis Cathaigh (Scattery Island in English) but firstly he travelled abroad, making the acquaintance of several other saints, including Aidan at Enniscorthy, and was befriended by Saint David, on passing through Menevia as many saints did coming to and from Ireland.

Senan visited Rome and the shrine of Martin of Tours in France and possibly on his roaming (although untold in his *Life*) founded the church of Sennen in south-west Cornwall. There are some occurrences of dedications to Senan or 'Sannan' in Wales such as at Llansannan, but like the Cornish parish, we cannot be sure if these originally related to a different personage of the same name. Senan was traditionally identified by Leland and others as the *Sinnin* who came across from Ireland to Cornwall in the company of Breaca, but Baring-Gould prefers Setna, a disciple of Senan's from Inis Mór (see Chapter 2).

Senan was seemingly fond of secluded islands. On returning to Ireland, he created monastic houses at a series of different *Inis* (islands): Iniscarra, Inisluighne, Inis Mór (Deer Island), and Iniscaorach (Mutton Island), but apparently none were quite right for him until he finally settled on Inis Cataigh (Scattery Island), which in some versions he had been prompted to by the Archangel Raphael. However, this location was not without problems as a fearsome creature called the Catach roamed the island, which Senan duly contended with and expelled. Following this a local chief, Mac Tail, laid claim to the island and tried to oust Senan from it, first sending Senan's own brothers to persuade or to evict him bodily, then by sending a druid to challenge Senan to a cursing match, and finally in person, all of which were unsuccessful. Mac Tail died shortly afterwards and was replaced by a much kinder ruler who granted Senan the land on which to settle. He blessed the island so that no man buried in its soil would go to Hell.

A notable story from his life is the coming of the elderly nun Cannera, who had received a vision telling her to go to end her days at Inis Cataigh and be buried there. However on her arrival she learned of Senan's strict rule against allowing women to set foot on the island and, despite her pleas, Senan was unmoving. Cannera, an early defender of equal rights, argued that Jesus died and was resurrected for women just as much as men. He consented to her being buried on the seashore which is where she lingered and died. Senan's actions may seem outrageous to the modern mind but it is thought that his reasoning lay in the belief in separating male and female monastic communities to avoid temptation, rather than in misogyny.

Senan had in fact founded a community of nuns at Killeochaille which was the site of his death, whilst on the way back from visiting the shrine of his old teacher Cassidus. It seems he had promised the nuns either the relics of a monk of Inis Cataigh to act as protection over their convent or that his own body might lay there 'in state' for a while but, on his death, when his disciples came to remove his body, the nuns argued that it should be buried where he lay on their lands. This did not happen and his bones were translated to Inis Cataigh, but the Sisters were granted the saint's thumb as a relic.

Senan died on 1st March, St David's Day, but he is remembered on the 8th, the day of his burial. He is considered by some to have potentially taken over the guise of a pagan river god for whom the river Shannon was named; the river in which Inis Cataigh lay, and the story of his defeat of the creature Catach may evidence the transference of more ancient traditions and stories into the Christian age.

Senara

Senara is patron of the tiny community of Zennor, near Land's End, Cornwall, and the legends associated with her reflect the curious nature of Zennor's remote setting. She is commonly believed to have originated from Brittany as Saint Azenor, although Orme states that the original church dedication was to *Sinar*, a male saint (2000: 233).

Azenor's story is told in the *Life* of her son, Budoc. She was the daughter of the King of Brest who was one day attacked by a serpent which sank its teeth into his arm and could not be dislodged, until Azenor offered up her breast to which the monster transferred its grip. Azenor immediately cut off her breast with the serpent attached and cast it into a fire; for her bravery and piety she was made whole again by God.

Following this she married the Count of Goëlo but fell foul of her jealous stepmother who convinced Azenor's father and new husband that she had been unfaithful, and had her condemned to be thrown into the sea in a barrel. The princess, who was four months pregnant, drifted on the waves and was sustained by the angels until she came to term; giving birth at sea, attended by a vision of Saint Brigid who assisted her. The *Life* tells that she washed up on Irish shores but Cornish tradition asserts that she first landed at Zennor, and the fact that her son, Saint Budoc, is also known throughout Cornwall and Devon supports her being there.

Other maritime legends surround the church of Zennor, particularly the story of the Mermaid of Zennor. In the folk tale, a mysterious woman in fine clothes attended the church, sitting at the back and listening to the singing of the parishioners. Nobody knew from whence she came but were struck by her beauty. She became obsessed with one particular man, Mathey Trewella, whose voice was the finest in the village. Waiting for him outside the church, she revealed her true nature to him and convinced him to come away with her to return to her watery home. Mathey and the woman were never seen again, except for a sighting out by Pendour Cove when a ship accidentally cast its anchor over the door of her home and the mermaid appeared to them to ask them to remove it so she could return to her husband Mathey and their children.

Some say the tale inspired the carving of a mermaid bench end which is now preserved as the curious 'Mermaid Chair' in the church and attracts many visitors. Others say the carving inspired the tale, but whatever the case, Senara has become so inextricably linked to the sea that she is often referred to as 'the Mermaid Saint' and religious medals of her even feature the image of a mermaid.

Sidwell

Sativola, or Sidwell in English, was an Exeter based patroness. David Nash Ford regards the name Sadfyl to be more accurate (earlybritishkingdoms.com). Both he and Baring-Gould presume her to have been identical with Sicofolia, who is mentioned in the life of Paul Aurelian as his sister, despite Paul's family originating from Wales rather than Dumnonia.

Her Life, recorded in the Exeter Legendarium of Bishop Grandisson was seen by Leland but did not survive. It tells how her wicked stepmother employed some mowers to behead the young virgin Sidwell with a scythe as a sacrifice to bring end to a drought. Where her head fell, a spring was elicited, although the implication is that this was due to her piety rather than through the success of pagan sacrifice. Nash Ford tells us that her head was cast into the well which had sprung up on the site and on the fourth night after the murder, resurrected her body and carried her head to the place where she desired to be buried, which became a site for miracles thereafter.

Almost identical accounts in late sources are told of Devonshire saint Ulrith and Dorset saint Jutwara (Aud) who are sometimes claimed to be her sisters; so either the stepmother had a prolific career in murder, or some duplication has occurred. .

Sidwell is well represented in Exeter, depicted in art holding a scythe and appearing in stained glass, rood carvings and even in a relief on a shopping centre in Sidwell Street. She is patron alongside another supposed sister, Wulvella, at Laneast although the dedication is late. The Saxon rendering of her name – Sidwell – is thought to derive from a conjunction of 'scythe' and 'well', her two most popular emblems.

Right: St Senara: Within this painting St Senara holds the story of the 'Mermaid of Zennor', which has become tied into her own legend, earning her the title of the 'Mermaid Saint'. Acrylic on canvas board (16in x 20in)

Tydful

Tydful was another daughter of the prolific progenitor of saints, Brychan, who gives her name to the town of Merthyr Tydfil, which means 'the martyr Tudful'. She was born to Brychan's wife, Prawst in c.435. Not much detail remains of her saintly life, but rather it is her death which makes the history books. Other than appearing in the genealogy lists, the only account of her appears in the *Iolo Manuscripts* which describes how she was killed by 'pagan Saxons' in either 460 or 480 whilst en route to visit her father in Brecon.

Brychan's heir, Rhain, raised an army against the Saxons in retaliation and drove them back but not before falling in battle himself. He was known as Rhain Dremrudd, 'the Red-eyed', perhaps denoting a fearsome nature. His name has been duplicated in the lists of the children of Brychan as Rhun, Rhawin and Rhaint, variously, but sources agree that he was killed by the Saxons at a bridge over the River Taff in Merthyr called Pont-y-Rhun. Authority passed to his young son, Nefydd, who took up the fight and drove the Saxons from their lands.

Although Tydful is generally regarded as a real historical martyr, the author of the *Iolo Manuscripts* is noted for occasionally embellishing, (and some even say faking), medieval records. Her feast day of August 23rd is not mentioned in any surviving texts earlier than the sixteenth century. She is patron of the church of Merthyr Tydfil, and also the little church of Llysworney near Cowbridge.

Winifred

Saint Winifred, or Gwenfrewi to give her her correct Welsh name, belongs to the seventh century in the locality of Holywell (Treffynnon), North Wales. Accounts of her life come from the twelfth century and are regarded as being of questionable historical value. Shrewsbury Abbey claimed the relics of Winifred and a Prior named Robert provides us with the most complete *Life*, claiming to have used a mixture of written and oral sources. Despite the rather shocking fact that she goes unmentioned in the works of famous medieval authors such as Bede, Gerald of Wales, Geoffrey of Monmouth and William of Malmesbury, Winifred's cult was actually surprisingly large, and had the potential to rival Saint David's. We may wonder just how did this saint escape the notice of the great writers and the genealogists of the time?

Winifred was the daughter of a petty king of Gwynedd, Tefydd, and of Gwenlo, sister of Saint Beuno. The holy man came to lodge with his family and requested a plot of land in exchange for teaching his young niece. Winifred's *Life* tells that one day when her parents were at Mass, a young lord who was passing through the village on a hunt stopped at their home for a drink and, finding the maiden alone, attempted to force himself upon her. Winifred escaped and fled towards the church of her uncle Beuno and the young lord Caradog gave chase. Winifred reached the chapel door but sadly the amorous lord caught up with her before she could throw herself on her uncle's sanctuary. Winifred still resisted his seductions so Caradog, in a rage, beheaded her, causing a spring to flourish from the spot where her head hit the ground. Hearing the commotion, Beuno came out and was horrified at the scene. He cursed the lord, causing him to melt in to the ground, and placed Winifred's fallen head back on her shoulders, bringing her miraculously back to life[121]. By way of thanks, Winifred would weave a cape and send it to Beuno each year, placing it on a stone which travelled down the river until it found her uncle, whilst remaining bone dry.

One of the *Lives* tells that she visited Rome whereas another states that she founded a convent at Beuno's church of Holywell where she remained for seven years. Another says that following this incident, Winifred left home and wandered from house to house of different saints but was turned away until she was accepted at the abbey of Gwytherin, which was under the rule of relatives Eleri and Theonia; where she rose to the rank of abbess on Theonia's death. She died at Gwytherin, fifteen years after her decapitation and resurrection. Her relics lay at Gwytherin until they were moved to Shrewsbury in 1138. En route the remains were rested at Woolston, Oswestry, which also claims a well that rose up by virtue of Saint Winifred. Her relics drew in visitors to Shrewsbury but only a finger bone was said to escape the Dissolution[122].

---

121 Some sources say the 'Gwen' part of her name came from the white line of scarring that remained on her neck following her resurrection, although 'Gwen' was a common prefix in Welsh names of the time meaning white or bright (Baring-Gould and Fisher 1907 vol.3: 190)

122 An account from Holywell tells us that Gwytherin was loathe to give up Winifred's relics to Shrewsbury and that only one monk betrayed the whereabouts of her body. He was poisoned and put in the coffin in her place, and given to Shrewsbury, whilst the monks of Gwytherin reburied their saint. However, two finger bones were left behind in the coffin, one of which eventually went to Holywell, the other remaining in the coffin with the treacherous monk (Breverton 2000: 289).

The well at Holywell, however, the site of Winifred's beheading, prospered past the Reformation and is still visited by large numbers of pilgrims to this day, up to 30,000 a year. It escaped destruction, it appears, because Henry VIII's grandmother was one of its patrons and commended the water's 'medicinal' properties. The shrine features a large star-shaped pool and flecks of red in the stone of the pool are said to be Winifred's blood. The flow of water today has been diverted; five times the volume used to flow through the pool in which people bathed. The site's popularity has earned it the name 'the Lourdes of Wales' by comparison, but it is actually one thousand years older than its rival!

Throughout history, a whole spectrum of pilgrims from peasants to kings visited the shrine, and its importance cannot be denied, being the only shrine to receive over 1300 years of unbroken pilgrimage. Despite her origins being cloudy and the authenticity of her life being speculative at best, Winifred's legend was powerful enough to maintain her cult. In 1415 the Archbishop of Canterbury commanded her feast day be held with as much importance as Saint David and Saint Chad, and Breverton adds this as evidence as to the prestige of her cult. Whereas David's evangelising was broad and covered South Wales, Winifred's was a niche cult and was contained to a small locality. Breverton suggests that this factor and the removal of her bones from Wales may have contributed to the fact that her fame never reached the same national heights as the cult of Saint David (2000: 285).

Appendices

Appendix 1

Feast Days of the Saints

Benignus	9th November
Beuno	21st April
Breaca	27th October
Brigid	1st February
Brychan	6th April
Brynach	7th April
Buriana/Bruinech	29th May
Cadoc/Cadog	25th September
Collen	21st May
Constantine of Dumnonia	9th March
Cleder/Clether/Clechre	4th November
Crewenna	1st February
Cuby/Cybi	8th November
Cyngar	27th November

David	1st March
Digain	21st November
Dunstan	19th May
Dwynwen	25th January
Dyfrig/Dubricius	14th November
Eiliwedd	1st August
Elwin	22nd February
Endelient	29th April
Erbin	13th January
Erc/Erth	31st October
Euddogwy/Oudoceus	2nd July
Euny/Uny	1st February
Geraint ab Erbin	16th May
Germoc	30th July
Gerran/Geraint	16th May
Gildas	29th January
Govan	26th March
Gwinear/Fingar	23rd March (Cornwall), 14th December (Brittany)
Gwynllyw	29th March

Gwladys	29th March
Helen/Elen	22nd May
Ia	3rd February
Illtyd	6th November
Indract	8th May
Joseph of Arimathea	17th March (Traditional Western), 31st July (Eastern), 31st August (New Roman)
Juliana	29th June
Just/Iestyn/Ust	12th April, 10th October (Wales), 14th August (Roseland), 1st November (Penwith)
Kananc/Canauc	7th October, 9th October
Kea	3rd October (Brittany), 5th November (Cornwall)
Kerhender/Cynidr	27th April, 8th December
Keyne/Cain/Kenwyn	8th October
Levan/Salamon/Selevan/Selyf	14th October
Maben	18th November
Melangell	31st January
Menfre/Minver	24th November

Merewenna/Marwenna	12th August
Michael	8th May (Apparition), 29th September (Michaelmas)
Morwenna	5th July, 8th July
Nectan	17th June
Neot	31st July
Non	2nd March, 3rd March
Patrick	17th March
Paul Aurelian	12th March
Petroc	4th June
Piala/Ciara	20th November, 14th December
Piran/Ciaran	5th March
Rumon/Ruan	30th August
Samson	28th June
Senan	8th March
Senara	6th May
Sidwell	31st July
Sinnin/Sithney/Sezni	4th August
Tedda/Teath	15th January

Teilo	9th February
Tudfyl	23rd August
Wenna ferch Brychan	18th October
Wenna ferch Cynyr	18th October
Winifred/Gwenffrewi	3rd November
Wymp/Veep	1st July

Appendix 2

The descendants of Constantine Gorneu

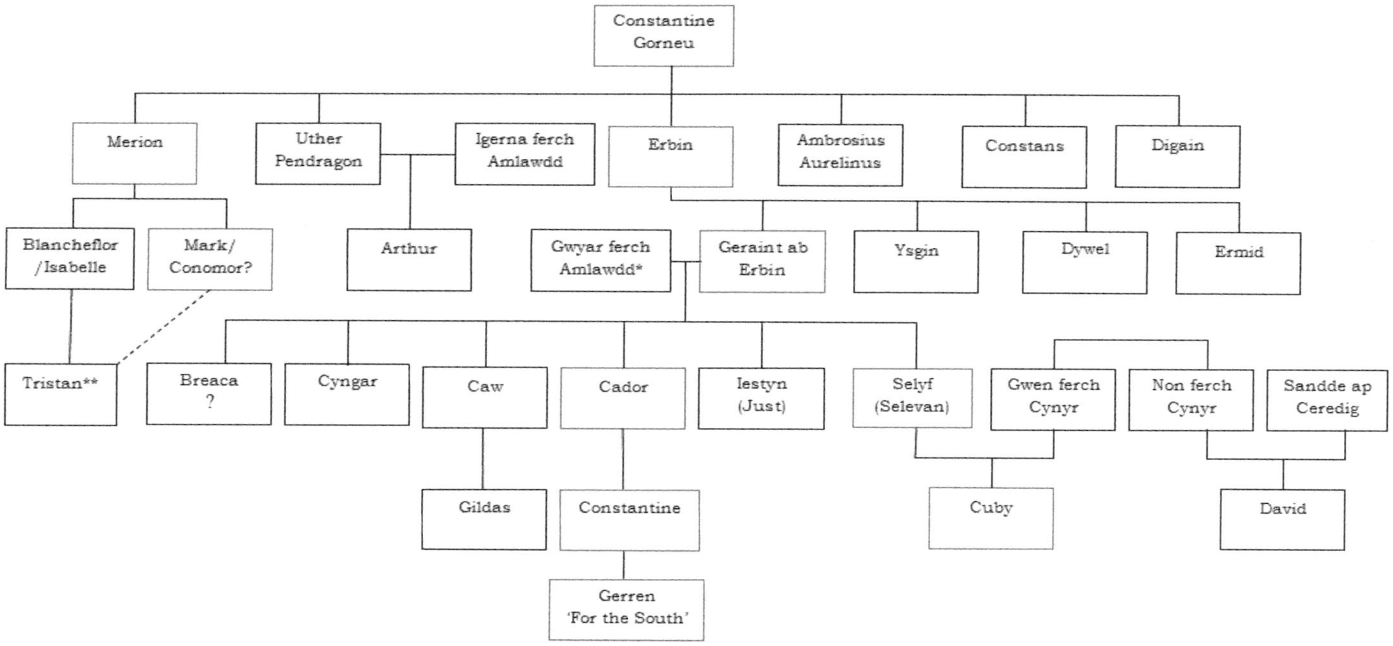

*Gwyar may only be mother of Cador, not all siblings

**Tristan may be nephew or son of Mark/Conomor

Bibliography

Barber, Chris & Pykitt, David (1997) *Journey To Avalon: The Final Discovery Of King Arthur.* Maine, Weiser

Baring-Gould, Sabine (1899) *A Book of Cornwall.* London, Methuen & Co

Baring-Gould, Sabine & Fisher, John (1907) *The Lives Of The British Saints* vols.1-4. London, John Hodges

Baring-Gould, Sabine (1914) *The Lives Of The Saints* vol.1-16. Edinburgh, John Grant

Baring-Gould, Sabine (1888) *The Vicar of Morwenstow: A Life of Robert Steven Hawker, M.A.* New York, Thomas Whittaker

Berresford Ellis, Peter (1974) *The Cornish Language and its Literature.* London, Routledge and Kegan Paul

Berresford Ellis, Peter (1992) *The Cornish Saints.* Penryn, Tor Mark Press

Bord, Janet & Colin (1972) *Mysterious Britain.* London, Garnstone Press

Breverton, Terry (2000) *The Book of Welsh Saints.* Vale of Glamorgan, Glyndŵr

Brighton, Simon & Welbourn, Terry (2010) *Echoes Of The Goddess.* London, Ian Allen

Cartwright, Jane (2008) *Feminine Sanctity and Spirituality in Medieval Wales.* Cardiff, University of Wales Press

Condren, Mary (1989) *The Serpent And The Goddess.* London, Harper & Row

Dark, Ken (2000) *Britain And The End Of The Roman Empire.* Stroud, Tempus

Davis, Courtney (1988) *The Celtic Art Source Book.* London, Blandford Press

Doble, Gilbert Hunter (1971, first published as separate booklets) *Lives of the Welsh Saints.* Cardiff, University of Wales Press

Drew, Samuel (1824) *The History of Cornwall: From the Earliest Records and Traditions, to the Present Time,* Volume 2. Helston, Penaluna

Flight, Edward G. (1871) *The Horse Shoe.* London, Bell & Daldy

Fortune, Dion. (2000, first published 1934) *Glastonbury: Avalon of the Heart.* Maine, Weiser

Freeman Johnson, Richard (2005) *St. Michael The Archangel In Medieval English Legend.* Woodbridge, Boydell & Brewer

Gasquet, Francis Aidan; Bishop, Edmund; & St Toke, Leslie Alexander Lawrence (1908) *The Bosworth psalter: an account of a manuscript formerly belonging to O. Turville-Petre, of Bosworth Hall,* now *Addit. ms. 37517* at the British Museum, London

Giraldus Cambrensis (1846, written c.1193) *Liber de Principis Instructione.* London, Anglia Christiana

Giraldus Cambrensis, Forrester, Thoma (trans) (1905, written c.1194) *The Itinerary Through Wales: and the Description of Wales.* London, George Bell & Sons

Gorman, George Cornelius (1820) *The History and Antiquities of Eynesbury and St. Neot's, in Huntingdonshire and of St Neot's in the County of Cornwall.* London, Lackington, Hughes, Harding, Mavor, and Jones

Harris, J. Henry (1906) *Cornish Saints and Sinners.* London, J. Lane

Hawker, Robert Steven (1870) *Footprints of Former Men in Far Cornwall.* Bodley Head, J.R. Smith

Hill, G. F. (1916) *Apollo and St. Michael: Some Analogies,* in *Journal of Hellenic Studies* 36:134-162

Hunt, August (2010) *King Arthur: Shadows in the Mist.* London, Avalonia

Hunt, Robert (1903) *Popular Romances of the West of England.* London, Chatto and Windus

Inman, Vanda (2005) *Legacy of a Cornish Saint - St Clether Holy Well and Chapel.* Dundalk, Write Space

Ivakhiv, Adrian J. (2001) *Claiming Sacred Ground.* Indiana, Indiana University Press

Jago, Rev. Christine. (1998) *The Wickedest Parish in Cornwall.* St. Buryan Parochial Church Council

James, Beryl (1993) *Tales of the Saints' Way.* St Agnes, Truran

James, David & Bostock, Simant (1996) *Celtic Connections.* London, Blandford

Jenkins, Simon (2008) *Wales – Churches, Houses, Castles.* London, Allen Lane

John, Catherine Rachel (1981) *The Saints of Cornwall.* Wadebridge, Lodenek Press

Leitch, Yuri (2011) *Gwyn: Ancient God of Glastonbury and Key to the Glastonbury Zodiac.* Glastonbury, Temple Publications

Lewis, Lionel Smithett (1924) *St. Joseph of Arimathea at Glastonbury or The Apostolic Church of Britain.* London, A.R. Mowbray and Co.

Lewis, Lionel Smithett (1925) *Glastonbury – Her Saints.* London, St Stephen's Press

Malory, Sir Thomas (1998, original c.1470) *Le Morte D'Arthur*. Oxford, Oxford University Press

Matthews, Caitlin (1989) *The Celtic Tradition*. Shaftesbury, Element

Matthews, John (1991) *A Glastonbury Reader*. Wellingborough, Aquarian

Matthews, John (editor) (1999) *The Celtic Seers' Source Book*. London, Cassell Illustrated

Mayhew Smith, Nick (2011) *Britain's Holiest Places*. London, Lifestyle Press

Mescal, Danile (1902) *The Story of Inis Cataigh: Scattery Island*. Dublin, O'Donoghue and Co.

Michell, John (1990) *New Light on the Ancient Mystery of Glastonbury*. Glastonbury, Gothic Image

Mildren, James (1989) *Saints of the South West*. Ilkley, Bossiney Books

Miller, Hamish & Broadhurst, Paul (1989) *The Sun And The Serpent*. Launceston, Pendragon Press

Morgan, Richard Williams (1938) *St Paul in Britain*. London, Parker

Mullins, Daniel J. (2002) *Early Welsh Saints*. Gwynedd, Llygad Gwalch Cyf

Nance, Robert Morton (1951) *St. Michael in Cornish Tradition in Michael,* Prince of Heaven. J M Watkins (reprinted by Chalice Well Press, 2013)

Nash Ford, David. (2005) *Early British Kingdoms*. www.earlybritishkingdoms.com Wokingham: Nash Ford Publishing.

O'Hanlon, John (1875) *Lives of the Irish Saints* vol.II. Dublin, J.Duffy

Orme, Nicholas (1996) *English Church Dedications: With a Survey of Cornwall and Devon*. Exeter, University of Exeter Press

Orme, Nicholas (2000) *The Saints of Cornwall*. Oxford, Oxford University Press

Pascoe, W. H. (1985) *Teudar - A King of Cornwall*. Dyllansow, Truran

Pennick, Nigel (1996) *Celtic Sacred Landscapes*. London, Thames and Hudson

Phillips, Andy (2009) *An Forth Keltek*. Redruth, Spyrys a Gernow

Polwhele, Richard (1816) *The History of Cornwall, Civil, Military, Religious, Architectural, Agricultural, Commercial, Biographical, and Miscellaneous,* Volumes 1-3. London, Michel & Company, Ptrs.

Rahtz, Philip & Watts, Lorna (1993) *Glastonbury Myth And Archaeology*. Stroud, Tempus

Rees, Elizabeth (2001) *Celtic Saints In Their Landscape*. Stroud, Amberley

Rees, Rice (1836) *An Essay on the Welsh Saints or Primitive Christians... Founders of Churches in Wales*. London, Longman, Rees, Orme, Brown, Green, and Longman

Seal, John (1995) *The Dark Age Saints of Somerset*. Somerset, Llanerch

Skeat, Walter W. (editor) (1871) *Joseph of Arimathie.* London, Trubner

Straffon, Cheryl (1998) *Fentynyow Kernow – In Search of Cornwall's Holy Wells.* Penzance, Meyn Mamvro

Tatlock, J. S. P. (1939) *The Dates of The Arthurian Saints' Legends,* in Speculum 14.3:345-365

Tomlin, E. W. F. (1982) *The Church of St. Morwenna and St. John The Baptist Morwenstow A Guide and History.* Morwenstow, E. W. F. Tomlin

Wallace, Martin (1988) *Celtic Saints.* Belfast, Appletree Press

Whitaker, John (1804) *The Ancient Cathedral of Cornwall Historically Surveyed,* vol.1-2. London, John Stockdale

Whitaker, John (1809) *The Life of Saint Neot, the Oldest of All the Brothers to King Alfred.* London, John Stockdale

Index

A

B

C

D

E

F

G

R

S

T

U

V

W

Y

PUBLISHED BY AVALONIA
www.avaloniabooks.co.uk

CPSIA information can be obtained at www.ICGtesting.com
Printed in the USA
LVOW05s0822200515

439189LV00006B/19/P